Glimpse of Gable: The Thirties.

By

Lachlan F. Hazelton.

Cover Photo: www.istock.com

(c) 2016 Lachlan Hazelton. Glimpse of Gable: The Thirties
All Rights Reserved.

National Library of Australia Cataloguing-in-Publication entry

Creator: Hazelton, Lachlan F., author. Title: Glimpse of Gable: the thirties / Lachlan Hazelton. ISBN: 9780958007511 (paperback)

Notes: Includes bibliographical references. Subjects: Gable, Clark, 1901-1960. Motion picture actors and actresses--United States--Biography. Motion picture industry--United States--History. Nineteen thirties.
Dewey Number: 791.43028092

www.trove.nla.gov.au

Disclaimer: While every effort has been made by the author/publisher to acknowledge the correct rights holder and/or source of material used in this book, the author/publisher apologises for any unintentional and accidental error or omission that may occur. The author/publisher will gladly make corrections for any subsequent edition of the book.

For M.L.M and Sunshine

Glimpse of Gable: The Thirties

Contents

Overview	7
Prologue 1901-1930	9
1930-1	20
1932	41
1933	56
1934	63
1935	71
1936	79
1937	90
The King 1938	94
Gable Rules	98
1939 Gone With The Wind	103
Select Bibliography	123
Glimpse of Gable Filmography	124
About The Author	126
Sources/Endnotes/ Image Credits	126

SB

For information on Glimpse of Gable: The Thirties, or to order copies go to

glimpseofgable@gmail.com

Other Titles by this Author

Team Work (2001)

Basic Brando (2005)

Film Favourites (2005)

Advertising & Small Business (2006)

Grandpa's Fish: A family tale (2007)

Family Feast (2010)

Wednesdays. A little book of Poems (2015)

Gracie. Our dog and some poems (2016)

The Circle R Ranch (2016)

Overview

The glimpse of Gable on screen has that something, elusive star quality captured by the camera. It's something that holds an audience. For as long as that connection holds you've found a star. Eventually, film fades and stars wane. Some forgotten, others will always be remembered.

Gable's energy combined with the studio formula to create a rugged male screen persona dependable in all situations. The third element crucial to enduring success, even with the Studio system at its peak, was something personal, private and genuine, something unique. Gable had it. Often, people discover the secret to personal success.

Life taught him to want something was not enough, if you work hard for it, really hard, you might get lucky. Gable grabbed his chances with both hands and rode them out. There were ups and downs, but for 30 years, if his name was on the program you knew what you'd get.

Gable was lucky to work in the time of the Studio system, using it to advantage. For some, that's reason to dismiss any ability he had as an actor. Happily, Gable himself was the first to admit that his abilities were limited.[i]

Surely, few would argue that the man from The Painted Desert (1931) was the same actor who charmed Claudette Colbert and audiences in It Happened One Night (1934) His ability and his knowledge of how to use it came with experience. Gables experiences, intentionally or not are reflected by his screen persona in the roles he was given, as well as later in the roles he chose.

Experience is key. His confidence in that ability was enough to turn a part he had approached with hate and fear, (Rhett Butler in Gone With The Wind 1939), into one of the greatest and enduring portrayals in Movie history. It was also personal experience and awareness that fuelled the nuance in the faded glory behind his outmoded Cowboy in Arthur Miller's The Misfits (1961).

Ideally, when he returned to a more relaxed work schedule after the birth of his son, this no nonsense experience would have coloured more parts, like the one that would have seen him teamed with John Wayne and Howard Hawks for Hatari (1962)[ii].

It would have made a productive and fitting Hollywood retirement. But, there isn't always the happy ending. (Gable died in November 1960). Paramount also balked at Gable's terms. They had trouble raising the budget to meet his $1 Million dollar fee, plus 10% of the box-office.[iii]

Yes, Clark Gable played Clark Gable. He never pretended to do anything else. Sometimes, his unique combination of personality, presence and persona gave his loyal audience a glimpse of something timeless.

Prologue 1901-1930

Just like the scenarios Louis B. Mayer was looking for in his films this one had it all, action, drama, romance. The scene would open with a long shot of a small farm, that despite all the work seemed to be permanently undernourished and needing more attention. When we move closer, the title card would read...

Cadiz, Ohio. 1901

William Gable was a hard man whose struggle with the elements on the farm yielded little success. Not one to give in he worked harder. The softer elements that drove him on were focused on Adeline, his resolute and radiant wife. The choices had not treated her well.

It's possible news she was expecting brought a flash of excitement followed quickly by ominous weariness for them both. As always, they would get through it.

So, one scene dissolves into another. Here William and Adeline clenched hands for a difficult birth. William Clark Gable was born on the first of February. Quickly out of danger, so William senior went back work, he knew that helped. Adeline quietly, slowly hoped to mend. Despite her efforts she silently surrendered when `Willy' was eight months old.

He was barely old enough to remember his mother and certainly not articulate enough to yet show how he resented that sappy name.

His father was not equipped for farming and nursing, so baby William was smartly farmed out to the in-laws. 1903 was a big year for Willie and his father. The farm was still a dirt patch, but there would be a new woman in their lives.

His father married Jennie Dunlap, a bright strong woman with a playful adventurous side. Willie found a playmate, as well as someone who would love and support him as a mother.[iv] (No matter what he got up to.)

By the time the family relocated to another farm at Ravenna Ohio, young Bill knew he wanted to get far away from farming. His father couldn't relate to him, you did your work and did as you were told period. When their battles turned physical, Jennie quietly and calmly reasoned on Bills' behalf. By sixteen he would do anything to get out.[v]

The out was dubious, there was a job in the rubber factory of Firestone tyres at Akron Ohio. With Jennie's support and his father vehement protests he went forward into the freedom of the unknown. How bad could it be?

Our story dissolves again, revealing the constant heat, sweat and grinding stench of daily shifts at the rubber factory. If he didn't find something to take his mind of it, he wouldn't last.

As luck would have it, he was drawn to the magical mayhem of the local music Hall. [vi] Compared to the factory it was paradise on earth. The carefree well-heeled lifestyle appealed to Gable so much that he began to spend every free moment there. Eventually, thanks to his persistence, he landed an unpaid job running errands. His ambitious imagination began to see a life in theatre unfold in his minds eye. Reality would soon intrude. Within a year he would be derailed by devastating news, Jennie was ill.

The loving son quickly returned home staying, despite the friction with his father, until she died. The tenuous tender connection to his old life was gone. There was nothing to hold him down.

His father, battered and beaten by the farm, sold up and hoped for better things courtesy of the Oil boom in Oklahoma.[vii] Young Bill hopped the first train out when his father suggested he join him.

A part did come his way, called The Jest. Brothers Lionel and John Barrymore were the headliners. Despite the optimistic title, there was little to smile at when the play quickly folded.[viii] Gritting his teeth he was forced to join his father on the oil fields. At $1 a day (12 hours), the 21 year old saw little future in it, quickly hitching up to another train.[ix] Back on his way to Broadway for his big break, he financed the journey with a succession of odd jobs. He did anything to keep on track, from lumber jacking to work in a department store.

Determined to make a go of it he stuck it out taking work where he could. He toured with a stock company in Kansas City, hoping to learn on his feet, but the company folded. There would be better luck with an Oregon Stock Company.[x] They were in a tight spot and needed someone quick. Once he signed on, he was in the thick of it. It was a blur of excited experiences. Josephine Dillon, a former actress of the New York Stage was drawn to the rugged charisma of this young newcomer.[xi]

Josephine would refine and focus his appeal. With diligent voice training he would learn to use the lower, sexier tones so appealing to his female audience. His no nonsense style, given added force. Finally, William, or `Billy' was nixed in favour of his stronger middle name, Clark.

By 1924 the relationship was founded on intimate mutual ambition. Dillon saw Hollywood as the next step, especially with her `star' discovery by her side.

In December they became husband and wife. He was 23, she was 37. There were a few unremarkable parts in films, but as a mute extra he made little impression. The refined grandeur of Silents, with it's taste for the urbane and alluring mystique of John Gilbert, or the action and romance of Douglas Fairbanks and Mary Pickford, had no room for the cumbersome Gable.[xii]

Soon the extra jobs dried up. With his father and the farm creeping back into view Gable spurred himself on.

Brushing shoulders with Lionel Barrymore in The Jest got him a small part in The Copper Head, again starring Lionel Barrymore.[xiii] The result was the same and Gable clung desperately to repertory theatre, grabbing a chance with a stock company in Houston Texas.[xiv]

The contract offered some form of security, so he could again focus on success. His masculine magnetism would again do the rest. While here, he caught the roving eye of Ria Langham. As Josephine before her, she saw the possibilities; his rugged virile male would provide her a welcome, satisfying distraction in the moneyed manicured society where she moved.

For Gable, there was the obvious physical attraction, but equally as strong, was his desire to attain all that Ria, with her polished and well moneyed sophistication, represented. Though still married to Josephine Gable and Ria became inseparable as he tried to break into Broadway. It was 1928, this time things would be different.[xv] The parts were better, just not the plays. Ria put her money where her mouth was and with her backing got him the plum lead role in The Last Mile (1930)[xvi]

It had made a star of Spencer Tracy, in fact Gable had been awe struck by Tracy's performance. Hopefully, Gable too would get lucky.

It was his breakthrough, in part thanks to his presence, but also thanks to Al Jolson. The Jazz Singer was a sensation when it hit cinema screens in October 1927, with Al Jolson talking his way into the history books. By 1928 the first complete talkie was shown, Lights of New York. Every studio was committed to sound. Warner Brothers had been the leader, but now other studios worked faster and faster to catch up.[xvii] MGM would soon be the new pack leader.

The old style of acting disappeared almost overnight, some stars failing to make the transfer because their voice didn't suit the public's view of them. Among the uncertain first steps of a new and vibrant Industry, everyone was looking for fresh new talent.

Two well-connected film men caught Gable in The Last Mile and recognised potent potential. One was Mervyn Leroy, a Director at Warner Brothers, the other Lionel Barrymore.

Both were impressed enough to ask he be screen tested, Mervyn at Warner Brothers and Lionel at MGM. Like his first foray into Hollywood in 1924 this second attempt soon hit a snag. Warner Brothers casting rejected him upon immediately citing his large ears.[xviii]

Then, although Lionel enjoyed a permanent place in Louis B Mayer's affections,(Always one of his favourites, he eventually enjoyed a lifetime contract.) his belief Clark failed to sway the talent spotters, there was no contract.

Undeterred, Gable took the next opportunity that crossed his path. It was in a William Boyd Western **The Painted Desert** (1931). This is where one Gable myth took hold, the fact that despite being raised on a farm and doing some Wildcatting with his father in the rough and tumble of the Oklahoma oil fields, he never could ride a horse. He was a good rider and easily impressed. Clark got the part.

The Painted Desert (1930)

This glum, laborious William Boyd western is hardly an auspicious start, but it did offer Gable his first speaking role. For the most part the dialogue and the actors are stilted and wooden, creaking like the first wagonload of ore from this frontier story. It's simple enough, two frontier men discover an abandoned baby boy, each lays separate claim to it and the movie centres on the feud between the two men. It is (naturally) complicated by Helen Twelvetrees as the young man's love interest. She is the daughter of the other man. Sabotage and action ensue.

Driven by hate the two men hurriedly face off in a duel, accidentally shooting the boy they both love so much.

Suddenly, seeing what they've done they realise the folly of their ways, the wedding goes ahead and the two families live happily ever after.

The fact that this happens in just 70 odd minutes adds to the bottom of the rung "B" Movie feel.

Clark Gable does well enough as the villain of the piece, the trademark gruff delivery is there, but he isn't yet confident enough in front of the camera. His Menace is up to the job in some scenes but not in others. A fine first effort. Definitely for Gable completists only.

On the strength of this performance, Lionel Barrymore persisted and arranged a second screen test at MGM. Reluctantly, Gable was signed to a 2 year contract with six monthly options, at $350 a week in 1930.[xix] For someone of such humble beginnings, it was unthinkable, when times were so hard, that he would be given that much money for doing almost nothing.

The uncertainty he felt was common for many who were sudden successful throughout the young Industry. The money for several weeks work on Painted Desert alone was an absolute fortune ($11,000) compared to the dollar a day slog of the oil fields.[xx]

Gable suspected nothing this easy would last, and he wasn't ever going back to Ohio, so he would be smart. Work hard for as long as it lasted and save for the day when this parade would get rained on.[xxi]

For some, success means always working. Throughout the 30's Gable took this to heart. Looking back over his entire career, this was to be his most confident, productive and popular period as a star for MGM. After an uncertain start he would be a prolific and profitable earner for the studio, releasing a dozen films in 1931 alone.

His most famous roles can be found in this period, so to can all the conspiring elements of his career success. This was, for both Gable and MGM, a golden age of dreams and possibilities. Through Gable the audience caught a glimpse of both.

1930-1931

The contract of $350 a week was a lot of money, with all the frantic excitement of the studio sound stage, Gable recognised the competitive streak in his fellow freshman. There was a high turn-over, even the big stars were only as good as their last picture.

He was just starting out, if he didn't catch their eye with hard work, he'd be out on his ear. He went to all the classes, learnt to ride a horse, dance, even sing. Every contracted actor attended their studio's image factory.

This was MGM, he was starting at the top. So, he'd have to work that much harder. Founded in 1924, MGM was the number one studio, it was built on Family Values and family entertainment. Louis B Mayer would sit at the head of this tinsletown table for thirty years as a stern but generous patriarch. Mayer had his own frantic formula for success as an independent producer when Metro Pictures Corporation and Goldwyn Pictures tapped him on the shoulder to oversee their grand plan.[xxii]

Late in 1923 Metro Pictures a venture of Marcus Loew, had suffered badly due to departures in management, but worse still was the decision of Rudolph Valentino not to renew his contract. Goldwyn Pictures was also suffering a bout of poor box-office. F.J. Godsol (Joe) had seized control from Sam Goldwyn to fight for survival, but he needed help. Both men saw a Life saving and potentially lucrative merger as the answer. A mutual friend suggested Mayer was the missing ingredient. Already known for his strong family oriented approach to even the most difficult stars, which brought him enviable results, it was decided. MGM was born.[xxiii]

Now the new Company was six and Talkies were only 3 and still finding their feet. Even now each Studio had a definite identity which sound could add a fresh dimension to. MGM was the family Studio. The reality of the early 30's was much darker than their wholesome fare. For many, the studio synonymous with the dirty dark reality of gangsters and hoods was Warner Bros.

Their pictures were not as glamorous, but they tapped into the harsh edge of the streets with some of the best Gangster films ever put in a can.

Gable really didn't warrant much attention from either Mayer or Irving Thalberg, who was Mayer's pressured, talented and ambitious chief of production. Possibly recalling his original reaction to his screen test, Thalberg saw Gable's rugged presence as best suited to other peoples pictures, but there were a few supporting opportunities.

At least they would earn some money until they decided what to make of him. Ironically, his imposing presence gave Gable his first screen success at Warner Brothers. Both Jack Warner and Darryl F. Zanuck had all but ignored him two years ago.

He did okay in **The Finger Points**, so they put him into a Barbara Stanwyk flick. **Night Nurse**, with Gable as the menacing rugged Limo driver Nick, he got everyone's attention. Stanwyk had top Billing, but the audience wanted to know about Gable.

Now, coupled with the chemistry between Crawford and Gable in **Dance Fools Dance** and public reaction to Night Nurse, MGM knew what they had and how to use it. Clark Gable had arrived.

Of course, Warner's would find their man in movies when Mae Clark wore a Grapefruit courtesy of the high caliber performance by James Cagney in **Public Enemy (1931)**
The Easiest Way (1931)[xxiv]

A beautiful young model finds the easiest way to support her family. As a well to do pretty plaything she finds all she could want.

This sudsy soap slips along until the woman in question (Constance Bennett) is slapped by true love by a genuine Mr. Nice Guy (Robert Montgomery) Will true love win the day!? Adolphe Menjou plays it cool and classy as Bennett's meal ticket. Gables name is on the support list in this one, Anita Page as Bennett's lively younger sister; and sturdy Clark Gable, as Page's laundry man boyfriend.

Dance Fools Dance. (1931) with Joan Crawford.

This is a Joan Crawford vehicle. She is clearly the star. Gable is menacing and suitably confident as the tough, charming and ruthless bootlegger. His supporting role is given added impact thanks to references to the character for the first 30 minutes. With such a great build up Gable makes the most of it, right from his first appearance. Crawford's star would continue to rise, but suddenly Gable was noticed by audiences and exec's alike.

The story is simple enough Bonnie Jordan (Crawford) is a good time girl from a wealthy family, popular and fun-loving. She loses her father and their fortune in the stock-market crash. It's a rude awakening, the popularity of her bank balance gone, she gets a job at a paper, The Star. After a shaky start Bonnie finds her feet thanks to Bert Scranton, a likeable fellow reporter.

She starts following the local gang wars and finds herself smack in the middle of the action. While Bonnie has been working hard, her brother Ronnie has taken a job with tough bootlegger Jake Luva (Clark Gable). When Scranton is killed the paper puts her undercover in Luva's organisation to find the murderer.

As the new Cabaret number at his club, Luva immediately takes an interest in her, sparks fly and Bonnie struggles to keep her distance as she gets further and further in. The tension spills over in a messy shot out in Bonnie's apartment after her cover is blown. Naturally, when the smoke clears Bonnie finds true love and lives happily ever after.

Thirties filming aside, the leads are fresh, the film stands up well, making good watching today. Crawford cuts a fine figure and sparkles throughout. Gable dominates every scene he's in. A Good place for a Gable collection to start.

Gable's strong masculine presence dazzled Crawford off screen and on. It wasn't long before she spent every possible moment at the Studio with him. The attraction was mutual.[xxv] Eager to exploit the chemistry, her next film Torch Song was quickly reshot with Gable replacing Johnny Mack Brown. Production was not going well and they saw firing Brown as a win win. The film was eventually released as **Laughing Sinners**.[xxvi]

The Finger Points. (1931) Warner Brothers

In this 30's Gangster flick News hound (Richard Brathelmess) crosses to the wrong side of the tracks. As a 'Finger Pointer' for the Mob he is fed stories that will help knock off their competition. Richard Brathelmess is the lead, Gable is again cast as the heavy, competent enough as the gangster.

Type casting appeared imminent as his popularity with audiences grew. Such was MGM's enthusiasm, that Gable was filming The Finger Points, Night Nurse and The Easiest Way at once.[xxvii]

The Secret Six. (1931)

Back at MGM he was again in gangster garb. This gangster film has a talented cast. Wallace Beery plays a Capone-like hood who doesn't let anything, or anyone stand in his way. Tax problems put his power and influence to the test, down but not out he struggles to reassert himself. Support cast includes Johnny Mack Brown, Clark Gable, Lewis Stone, Ralph Bellamy and Jean Harlow.

Wallace Beery had a prickly personality at the best of times, often disliked by those who spent time with him. He was a violent drunk, especially with his wives.[xxviii] (Gloria Swanson first and now Rita Beery)

The public loved his likable lug image onscreen, which MGM did it's best to maintain.[xxix] At 44 he had worked in Silents for many years, before being discarded with the coming of sound. Mayer and Thalberg took him on, making good use of him in **Min and Bill (1930)** with Marie Dressler, before **The Champ** with Jackie Cooper. He was totally uncouth, ignored most of his scripted dialogue.

Most of his antics were tolerated thanks to enduring box-office. He would prove a top asset to the established Gable, clashing well in the high caliber productions of **Hell Divers** and **China Seas**. Other highlights include **Grand Hotel (1932)** and **Dinner at Eight (1933)**. By the Forties time and his temperament slowed him down, before drink delivered a fatal heart attack in 1949.[xxx]

Laughing Sinners (1931) with Joan Crawford

With this film their passionate attraction finally exploded on set, though clandestine, MGM did not want a scandal, no matter how good the box- office.

Gable had only just married Ria, while Crawford was Cinderella to Douglas Fairbanks Jnr, prince of Hollywood.[xxxi] Thalberg hoped separating them for their next few projects would through enough cold water on the situation.

Jilted Josephine was not surprised when she was a victim of the same ambition that first brought them together. The unexpected twist in the scenario was not a younger woman, but an older one. Gable had dropped her like a hot potato in 1928, but things had been so hectic, the divorce wasn't final until March 1931.

Gable hastily married Ria, the Bride was 47, Groom 30.[xxxii] The amorous association with Miss Crawford had already taken hold, as he strode up the isle. Problems were for other people, Clark was on the up and up.

For what it's worth the story for **Laughing Sinners** is pure Hollywood fluff, in fact some of the dialogue brings a hearty laugh as you almost choke on a massive cornball, but it hardly seemed to bother audiences.

Gable suits up for the Salvation Army and struggles to keep energetic Crawford on the straight and narrow. She runs afoul of Neil Hamilton's charms, seen here as a young, handsome, but heartless playboy. (In his next life he would be Commissioner Gordon to Adam West's Batman.) It's up to Clark to keep her from sliding back into trouble.

A Free Soul (1931) with Norma Shearer and Lionel Barrymore[xxxiii]

Here Gable found familiar faces. First there was Lionel, who had known him briefly through his stage work, before catching him in The Last Mile and going to bat for him with Mayer and Thalberg. The other, Leslie Howard, had the opposite opinion of his early career, but they remembered with a smile just the same.[xxxiv]

Leslie Howard had met Gable as a struggling actor round about a year ago. He was auditioning wherever he could, hoping for that big break. Gable thought a small part in Out of a Blue Sky was about his speed.

The play had been adapted from German by Leslie, who also wore the director's hat. There were quite a few possibilities for the part described simply as German Play reader. Leslie let this brooding young man with big ears soldier on, but he and his stage manager were hoping for something softer, so Gable missed out.[xxxv]

The free soul of the title is Norma Shearer who is an independent woman on the outer with her well to do socially respectable family. Her free spirit been fostered by her father (Lionel Barrymore).

His performance as a lawyer on the slide, propping himself up with a bottle before finally falling in, still resonates today. The character's self awareness is given a wonderfully subtle humanity. His enduring love for his daughter is enough to give him one more impassioned day in court, valiantly arguing for her life, attempting to make amends.

Gable is Ace, a well connected Gangster Barrymore gets off a murder wrap. At his trial he meets and sets his sights on Norma Shearer.

Sparks fly as she is dazzled by Ace's world. So dazzled is she, that poor ever respectful Leslie Howard (Champion Polo player no less!) is cast aside. So devastated is the jilted lover, that he confronts Ace at gunpoint. It is vintage melodrama, dated by tedious dialogue and the morality of the time in spots. Barrymore manages to steal each scene he's in (walking of with the award for best actor). Gable and Shearer have a timeless energy together that makes this rainy day Midday Movie fare.

Night Nurse (1931) Warner Brothers

By the time this Barbara Stanwyck vehicle was released Gable was as well known as Stanwyck. It reminded Warner's that they had let this star slip away. His part in the film didn't reflect his rise in stature, but his energy keeps his scenes fresh in the mind long after you forget the rest.
The film should belong to sassy Stanwyk, who charms her way into a nurses job. Nurse Hart (Stanwyk) is helped by equally rebellious and playful Joan Blondell, together they manage to have some fun under the hospital matrons ever prying nose.

Naturally, they also manage to uncover a plot to kill to children and claim their lucrative trust fund. A girls gotta do what a girls gotta do. Nurse Hart stands up to the rough and ready Chauffeur Nick (Gable) who is the mind and muscle behind the scheme. His scenes have more intensity than those of the main stars, he keeps the film together before being taken for a ride and meeting a nasty end.

Ben Lyon (Howard Hughes' **Hells Angels** 1930) is the likeable bootlegger pal who has a soft spot for Nurse Hart, always managing to get her out of trouble. It is likable, but Gable is the real standout.

Sporting Blood[xxxvi] (1931) first starring role

Gambler Rid Riddell (Gable) wins a racehorse, Tommy Boy, on a bet. Rid consistently wins with the horse in fixed and legit races. As he starts to realise success things are naturally complicated by girl, in this case the Trainer's daughter.

Despite what she knows about Rid they fall in love and through her he sees the error of his ways. He wants to marry her with a clean slate, so he lays plans (with her secretly helping him too) to get out from under the mob. Naturally all ends well. There is plenty of Horse racing action in this film, using popular tracks and other names of the day yet watched today it all seems static and uninspired. For his debut as lead Gable seems conspicuous by his absence most of the time.

This film was a hiccup in Gable's rapid rise to the top ranks at MGM. It was a successful maiden voyage as the main star, but detractors pointed out his box office receipts were not as good as expected. Gable was a passing fad, not a good long-term investment. Irving Thalberg was now in Gable's corner and insisted on keeping him. The powers that be were confident his popularity would rebound. That, plus Greta Garbo selecting him to star opposite her in her next film was enough to silence the critics.[xxxvii]

To be fair, less than anticipated box office should really have been expected, releasing 12 films in 1 year is almost too much of a good thing, even for the most dedicated fan.

Susan Lenox (Her fall and Rise) (1931) Co-star to Greta Garbo[xxxviii]

Greta Garbo the mysteriously seductive Swede was imported from Berlin by MGM at 19 after Mayer had been impressed by he work. She managed to hold out for a lucrative contract, signing in January 1925.[xxxix] Garbo was often nervous, unfeeling and aloof in person. Film was her best form of expression because of the controlled nature of it. Garbo would often assert herself to the detriment of studio schedules and her starring vehicles. While her popularity held, these were tolerated. The mystique of legend was partially devised perhaps to limit her exposure to interviews, lest the press and audience discover an unvarnished truth. Whatever her insecurities or inadequacies, her screen performances mesmerised and rose above everything.

By 1931 the screen goddess/prima donna had taken hold. Her knowledge of her own position only made her more difficult to bring to heel.[xl] Her appetites and arrogance were unassailable. With such unprecedented control and choice of material. Garbo was not bound to anything like the output that Gable and others were. From 1932 she would make less than a film a year. When she committed to the project her demands and quest for her own perfection meant the usual delays. The script was a major sticking point. Despite Fourteen writers labouring over the story, the result was only an adequate rehash of a common theme.[xli]

The stars too, found no common ground, in fact each approach was completely foreign to the other. Garbo could not relate to him and as a result felt her performance awful, while he had no time for her attitude, thinking her 'boring'[xlii]

Gable learnt from her in another way, seeing her enviable control over the set and her choice of material.

Always keen to protect what he had, when she walked off the set half a dozen times over the script, it showed him an effective bargaining tool that, once established, he could use to advantage.

Another clause saw her workday end punctually at 5pm. No matter what. Gable, enduring a grueling schedule, being part way through his sixth feature for MGM, would file that away for a future contract of his own.[xliii]

It also irritated him that despite his continued protests, Gable tolerated the MGM make-up men taping his ears back, after all he'd only just started in this business, better not push it. Thankfully, In the middle of a key scene with Garbo, one of his ears sprang out. Number crunchers noted the costly re-shoots that would be needed each time. The scene was re-shot but the studio never touched his ears again.[xliv]

Midday melodrama again here. Helga (Garbo) is the unwanted child of a down and out family. Clever use of shadows shows her growing up in as the abused servant girl to her Uncle. Forced into an arranged marriage with the lout of a neighbour (Alan Hale), all seems lost. She runs out into a storm when the drunken neighbour forces himself on her. Whose garage should she seek refuge from the elements in?

Rodney (Gable) naturally persuades her inside. Of course, with such a kind man, thanks to the idyllic surroundings she lets her guard down just in time for this idealistic young engineer to jump on a train with hopes of winning a competition to make his fortune.

Returning home, once again she runs afoul of the evil uncle and co. She jumps onto a carnival train passing Lennoxville and thanks to the tattooed lady, she becomes Susan Lennox.

Susie manages to fall in with the wrong fella while avoiding Uncle. Rodney finds her and takes it badly. Devastated, she dedicates herself to being a good time girl and Rodney slides further into a bottle to forget her. The story follows the title the rest of the way as our heroine goes ups and downs ad nauseam infinitum. Finally they reunite on the lowest rung and she promises to rebuild their life together. There are first class elements at work here, but it seems to surrender to disinterest in the middle, the reunion at the end tries to recover lost ground. Such a lot of work for only okay returns. Garbo and Gable never worked together again.

Possessed (1931) with Joan Crawford.[xlv]

By the time this film rolled around Crawford was firmly established as a sultry star of sound, yet she had been busy in films for much longer, already having 22 silent films under her belt. Here is the established and formula for a Joan Crawford picture. Wide eyed country girl goes after a bigger life. Naturally, there's the usual complications.

For this outing Marian (Crawford) works in a hot sweaty paper box factory, it's located in an equally uninteresting town. Naturally, there's a well meaning dependable guy who gets the short end of the stick (Wallace Ford). She catches a contagious glimpse of the good life a party train rests for a moment at the local station. There she talks to Wally Stewart ('Skeets' Gallagher), who blissful and bleary eyed slips her his card.

She turns up card in hand during one of Wally's sober moments. After he lets her in on the realities of the big smoke, she orchestrates her own introduction to Mike Whitney (Clark Gable, headlining the support cast) an ambitious wealthy and well connected lawyer who is on the rise in State politics.

The good time is tarnished by Whitney's previous bad marriage and the messy very public divorce. Marian suffers in silence, even assuming another name, as a divorced socialite. The charade cracks when small town Al seeks her out, armed with larger ambitions. It collapses completely when Whitney is asked to run for Governor, the only pre-requisite being no Marian. He refuses so Marian sacrifices herself. The final political rally brings it all to a head nicely.

Will they or wont they? The question proved tantalising to audiences, giving them a huge hit. Off screen their liaison lit up her dressing room, (which husband Doug Jnr. was still paying for) or anywhere else they could steal a private moment at the studio.[xlvi] Fearing it would soon spill over onto front pages nationwide, the studio again went into damage control. By the time this was released it was a thinly veiled Industry secret, yet both spouses were oblivious. Once again, both were hurriedly dispatched in different directions.

Hell Divers (1932)[xlvii]

There is certainly enough action, in the form of complete co-operation from the Navy, to keep Gable busy and out of any trouble off the set. Even today the action sequences lose little edge, softened only by the nostalgia of antiquated technology and equipment. Naturally, this gives the film another enjoyable element, historical value.
The story is a fast paced mix of flying and fighting. There is a glimpse of a girl, but that's about it. It makes great use of both Gable and Beery who was also at his best box office wise.

The story starts off at a Navy training camp where top dog Chief Windy Riker (Beery) losses his customary 1st place in air gunnery training to younger and faster Nelson (Gable) This sets up the antagonism between the two for the film. Riker is coming up to mandatory retirement and finally settling down with his dependable sweetheart Mame.   Thinks go awry when his understanding C.O. is grounded after losing an arm while perfecting the new risky new dive bombing of the title, Riker gets into more and more trouble as he tries to out do Nelson wherever possible. Hostilities between the two reach breaking point when Riker torpedoes Nelsons marriage plans. Mame almost manages to get them to sort things out over a beer, but they end up in a brawl.

Naturally, risky training exercises in Panama add to the tension. Nelson's plane goes down in the fog, then Riker's follows when they botch a rescue of their own. The two men reluctantly bond and make a perilous dash for the Carrier in their damaged plane. The aerial sequences coupled with the production's sweeping access to Carriers and all Naval hardware mean the action is realistic and watchable, with the actors, on occasion, happily in the backseat. It all combined for blistering box-office.

So, he finished the year on a high note. Gable had weathered the studio doubts about his long-term box office, after the doubts over Sporting Blood, but the uncertainty and insecurity never completely left him. It was a rough road to get here, he didn't want to go back. The pressure of such a hectic schedule in 1931 was soothed by Crawford and complicated by Ria (or visa versa). Success, he hoped, would make things easier. This was hard.[xlviii]

" I worked three months straight without a day off. If this is what it's like being a success, when will I have a chance to enjoy it?"[xlix]

Bouyed by the firm box-office ground beneath his feet, he felt justified in asking for a pay rise. His personal life may have been tiring; he would see to it that work didn't have to be. Mayer, a masterful actor himself was thrilled to talk to him, eager to impress upon him how thrilled he was with his success. But everyone had to be mindful of how hard it was for people everywhere, especially in the motion picture business. Times were hard and Mayer struggled to keep it all together. In such testing economic times an extra $50 a week was the best he could do.

Fine. Gable left quietly. Sure, he should have told him what for, but he didn't want to push it. After all, there was plenty about this that he liked. The New angle Howard (Strickland) and the publicity boys came up with suited him down to the ground, the rugged outdoors, plenty of hunting and fishing. That was his idea of fun anyway, being just one of the guys. In-fact, as the Studio discovered and incorporated his strengths into the Gable image, he too would come to know his strengths as an actor, tirelessly perfecting them. Soon, with his growing confidence and application in front of the camera, image and actor would merge. William, the big eared boy from Ohio knew who he wanted to be when he grew up, Clark Gable.

The farm boy within would keep him firmly on the ground, always thankful, yet wary of fame and success. The caution is probably best applied to his approach to money. Despite the financial security of a bankable name, Gable never splashed his money around, distrusting banks and investments. Generous to friends and family, he developed the habit of carrying large amounts of cash around as a permanent safety net against any financial disaster.

Conversely, this attitude also meant disgruntled waiters, ex-wives and the like retaliated with stories of short arms and long pockets. Simply, he had been poor, and didn't like it. His confidence in his abilities (and his box office standing) meant he would take a different approach when he brought up his pay rise again, he'd try again in the New Year.

Before moving on to another busy year, there was as always, the annoying round of appearances expected from all the top stars at this time of year. One essential engagement was the annual New Years Day brunch at Mayer's beach house that he added to the Studio's social calendar four years previous. With $12 Million profit for 1931, MGM had reason to celebrate. The guest list this year had enough potential for a spectacle of a different sort.

Gable was on the guest list attending with his ever-territorial wife Ria, while Joan Crawford attended on husband Doug Fairbanks Jnr's arm. Given Gable and Crawford were still in the throws of passion between takes, their interactions this would have made for interesting viewing.

While the party passed quietly and occasionally awkwardly, Gable was not about to forget his request for a pay rise. Nor would he forget his grueling schedule for 1931. With his increasing confidence, both would have to change.

Gable didn't have a chance to catch his breath, as he got word he was expected on the set of the new Marion Davies vehicle. **Polly of the Circus**. Right. After one day of filming, there was still no word on his pay request. He now reasoned that he must be worth at least $10,000 as a draw card, even more with his cache of correspondence from captivated females. He figured his $650 a week was now up to $1000 or more.[1]

Day two dawned on the set of this fanciful fairy floss and he pulled a no show. This too, was a tactic Mayer was accustomed to. If anything, with Gable's output for the past year, he was surprised he lasted this long. Even so, his demand was more than reasonable, but Mayer had a reputation to maintain. That, plus he liked putting on a good show.

There was a series of late night - early morning emergency meetings between his agent and MGM brass to resolve the deliberate deadlock. Nothing. At one point William Randolph Hearst, unaccustomed to not getting his own way, barged in and said he'd throw in the best car he could buy. Gable returned to work for $2000 a week over 2 years from January 22nd 1932. [li]

Polly of the Circus (1932) with Marion Davies.

This is a fairly implausible undertaking, but with Gable's popularity that barely mattered. It was a vehicle for Marion Davies whose career was managed, manipulated and meticulously manufactured by William Randolph Hearst. His developing friendship with Mayer meant a comfortable partnership when Hearst's Cosmopolitan Pictures (formed exclusively to ensure his mistresses' stardom) was looking for a new partner. Davies sweet nature and generous disposition appealed to Mayer so much that he managed to tolerate her affair with Charlie Chaplin. [lii]

She successfully made the transition to sound and managed several endearing and engaged performances before being trapped by Hearst's (well intentioned) strong hold on her career. This storyline is implausible in the extreme, but there were the usual high production values and expensive set pieces, all to highlight Marion Davies.

Even on it's release, it must have seemed overblown an implausible, as circus aerialist Polly (Davies) has a fall from a great height and becomes smitten with the overly earnest clergyman (Gable) who put her up during her recovery.
This causes all manner of grief before being resolved, with the happy couple somersaulting over all obstacles. Time has not helped, Marion's restrained performance seems to come off as wooden. Gable seems ill at ease, miscast, yet they soldier on eagerly awaiting the end credits, perhaps as much as the audience.
The review in the New York Times March 19, 1932, describes some of the situations as "Ludicrous"[liii] This was part of the career slide for Marion, though through little fault of her own. Gable, known to enjoy his cars, may have disliked this vehicle, but he would have appreciated the current model Rolls Royce that Hearst offered him as carrot to return to work.[liv]

Red Dust (1932) Iv

Red Dust is a 1932 romantic drama film directed by **Victor Fleming** and starring **Clark Gable**, **Jean Harlow**, and **Mary Astor**. The film is based on the 1928 play of the same name by **Wilson Collison**, and was adapted for the screen by **John Mahin**.Red Dust is the second of six movies Gable and Harlow made together. More than twenty years later, Gable would star in a **remake**, **Mogambo** (1953), with **Ava Gardner** starring in a variation on the Harlow role and **Grace Kelly** playing a part similar to one portrayed by **Mary Astor** in Red Dust. The film, which is set in **French Indochina**, provides a view into the French colonial rubber business. This includes scenes of **rubber trees** being tapped for their sap; the process of coagulating the rubber with acid; native workers being rousted; gales that can blow the roof off a hut and are difficult to walk in; the spartan living quarters; the supply boat that arrives periodically; a rainy spell that lasts weeks; and tigers prowling in the jungle. The film's title is derived from the large quantities of dust that are stirred up by the storms. In 2006, Red Dust was selected for preservation in the United States **National Film Registry** by the **Library of Congress** as being "culturally, historically, or aesthetically significant".

The story is simple enough, on a rubber plantation in **French Indochina** during the monsoon season, the plantation's owner/manager Dennis Carson (**Gable**), a **prostitute** named Vantine (**Harlow**), and Barbara Willis (**Astor**), the wife of an engineer named Gary Willis (**Raymond**) are involved in a **love triangle**. Carson abandons an informal relationship with Vantine to pursue Barbara, but has a change of heart and returns to Vantine.

Vantine arrives at the plantation first, **on the lam** from the authorities in **Saigon**. She displays an easy comfort in the plantation's harsh environment, wisecracks continually, and begins playfully teasing Carson as soon as she meets him. He resists her charm at first, but soon gives in, and they quickly develop a friendly, casual relationship in which they tease each other and pretend to be too tough for affection. One of their favorite games is to call each other "Fred" and "Lily", as though neither can be bothered to remember the other's name. However, Carson loses interest in Vantine when the Willises arrive. Gary Willis is a young, inexperienced engineer, and his wife Barbara is a classy, ladylike beauty.

Carson is immediately attracted to Barbara, and, after sending Gary on a lengthy surveying trip, he spends the next week seducing Barbara as Vantine watches jealously. He successfully persuades Barbara to leave Gary for him, but recants after visiting Gary in the swamp and learning how deeply he loves Barbara. Carson has also seen that Barbara is unsuited for the primitive conditions on the plantation, as is Gary, and he has a painful memory of his own mother's death on the plantation when he was a boy. He decides to send both of them back to more civilized surroundings. At the story's climax, Carson turns Barbara's feelings against himself by pretending that he never loved her, at which point she shoots him. This provides a cover for Vantine and Carson to save Barbara's marriage and reputation by insisting to Gary that Barbara rejected Carson's advances. The film ends after Carson has sent the Willises away, with Vantine reading bedtime stories to him as he recuperates from the gunshot wound and tries to grab her.

Red Dust (1932) Gable watches Harlow with Victor Fleming directing

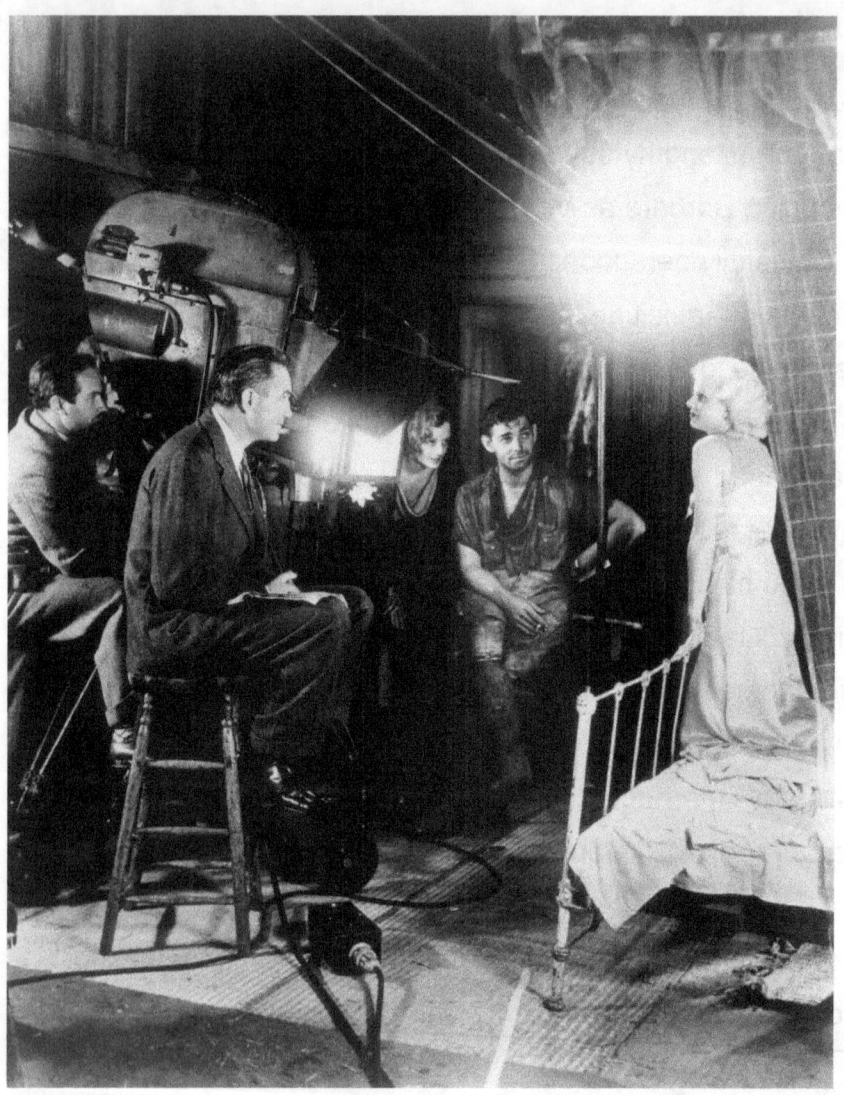

This film permanently cemented Gable's specific masculine ideal for cinema audiences. On the strength of it's box-office Clark Gable would find himself amongst the top 10 money earners. Gable, gentlemanly as always, would sit most comfortably at number two, when over taken by pint-sized crowd pleasers Shirley Temple and Mickey Rooney, or the comedy antics of Abbott & Costello. Gable would stay at number 2 until his distinguished war service in 1942.
He had held that position for 11 straight years. With his film the transformation was complete. From farm boy and wildcatter, to jobbing theatre actor and movie extra and now box office star. His new self-assured rugged masculinity found its most articulate expression here.
MGM deserves credit for finding the image to fit his style and qualities. Gable himself had his eyes on the prize too. Strong work ethic, diligent work on improving himself as an actor. His first two wives played their part too. The image was Gable's now, and he would always work to preserve its appeal. Where he needed to, he would protect it too. It was a winning formula. A formula that would essentially not change in 30 years.

No Man of her Own (1932) With Carole Lombard

This starred **Clark Gable** and **Carole Lombard** as a married couple in their only film together, several years before their own legendary marriage in real life.[lvi]

Gambler Babe Steward (**Clark Gable**) is in trouble with the law and decides to lie low in a small town. There he meets librarian Connie Randall (**Carole Lombard**) and attempts to seduce her. They flip a coin to decide whether or not to get married. The coin forces them to get married and Connie soon falls in love with Babe. Babe, meanwhile, continues his conning while telling Connie that he is working on Wall Street.

Connie does not suspect anything until she finds Babe's marked cards in his desk. She shuffles the cards and when Babe plays a game of poker, he loses. Babe wants nothing more to do with Connie and leaves for Rio de Janeiro to win big money at cards. But, realizing that he loves Connie, he gives himself in to the police to serve his jail sentence.

Babe returns to a pregnant Connie, he does not suspect that she knows of his deception, but she does not say a word about it and in true Hollywood fashion, we are left to assume that the couple lives happily ever after.

Miriam Hopkins was originally offered the lead, but balked at the idea of Gable receiving top billing, and demanded another project. Lombard, who was a rising star on the Paramount lot, but still relegated to roles in which she was second-billed to her male counterparts, was chosen to replace Hopkins.

During filming, Gable and Lombard were entirely indifferent to one another. On the last day of filming, Gable presented Lombard with a pair of ballerina slippers with a card attached that said, "To a true primadonna." Lombard got him back when she presented him with a large ham with his picture on it.[lvii] Gable kissed her goodbye and they did not stay in touch. It was not until four years later that their romance began to take off. Gable and Lombard never appeared together in another film, primarily because they became major stars at different studios, which didn't like to lend them out.[lviii]

Strange Interlude (1932) with Norma Shearer

1932 saw profits plummet across the boards everywhere. MGM was alone immune posting the indecent profit of $8 Million. It was a credit to the caliber of MGM's Star Roster. Thankfully MGM had Comedians as too, ensuring Depression ravaged audiences helped them laugh all the way to the bank.[lix]

This one creaks a lot when watching it today. On the face of it, all the elements are there for a hit. Great cast, plus Eugene O'Neill's play. Audiences were drawn to the stars easy enough, but plays can be hard to adapt.[ix]

In this case, the long ponderous deep and all too philosophical character asides were shoe horned into thoughts by the characters, delivered on the soundtrack during the scene. It was always going to be a challenge for a movie to pay effective and engaging homage to a five-hour play.[lxi] No element really works, so the film doesn't gel. The stars meant the box-office was good, but this exercise in art for art's sake didn't provide the dividends expected. It was at best, a valiant attempt.

The White Sister (1933) with Helen Hayes

The White Sister[lxii] is directed by Victor Fleming. It was based on the 1909 novel by F. Marion Crawford and was a remake of the silent film, The White Sister (1923), starring Lillian Gish and Ronald Colman.

Melodrama 101 here, Italian aristocrat Angela Chiaromonte (Helen Hayes) spurns the potential husband chosen by her father (Lewis Stone) in favor of Giovanni Severi (Clark Gable), a handsome army lieutenant. When her lover is reported killed in World War I, Hayes renounces the world to become a nun.

After she takes her vows, the lieutenant shows up very much alive. He implores her to give up the order, but she refuses. The lieutenant is later injured in a bombing raid; he dies, with Angela lovingly at his side.

Hold Your Man (1933) with Jean Harlow

Cinema ticket sales were in free fall in 1933. Cuts helped stop the bleeding. Even with revenue at it's lowest since the lion first roared in 1924, they were well ahead of the pack.[lxiii] Con man Eddie Hall runs from the police into Ruby Adams' apartment and she falls in love with the guy. Written specifically for both Gable and Harlow by Anita Loos, audiences responded to the realistic characters and crackling dialogue, giving an average plot spark at the box office.[lxiv]

Night Flight (1933)

Night Flight is a 1933 American aviation drama film produced by David O. Selznick and distributed by Metro-Goldwyn-Mayer and directed by Clarence Brown. The film stars the brothers Barrymore, John and Lionel, with Clark Gable and Helen Hayes.[lxv] With both the Barrymore prestige and the Gable clout, plus an award-winning novel filled with grim realism, it had the makings of another hit. John

Barrymore, snapped up by MGM when his contract with Warner's ended, had justified his $150,000 per film contract with a hit as suave thief in **Arsene Lupin** (1932)[lxvi]

It is based on the 1931 novel of the same name which won the Prix Femina the same year, by French writer and pioneering aviator Antoine de Saint-Exupéry.[lxvii] Based on Saint-Exupéry's personal experiences while flying on South American **mail** routes, Night Flight recreates a 24-hour period of the operations of the fictional airline, Trans-Andean European Air Mail. It is considered one of the most realistic aviation films ever filmed.[lxviii]

The plot was full of action and drama. In South America, the daunting mountains and dangerous weather have hampered the operations of Trans-Andean European Air Mail, a 1930s-era airline. Charged with delivering a serum to stem an outbreak of infantile paralysis in Rio de Janeiro, Auguste Pellerin (Robert Montgomery) conquers his fears, but is reprimanded by the airline's stern director, A. Riviére (John Barrymore) for coming in late.

Determined to make the night flight program work, Riviére has sent pilot Jules Fabian (**Clark Gable**) and his wireless operator on another dangerous flight. The pair become caught in a torrential rain storm and when Madame Fabian (**Helen Hayes**) comes to the headquarters, she realizes that her husband is overdue.

The two airmen, flying blind over the ocean, run out of fuel and choose to jump but are drowned. Riviére refuses to quit and orders a Brazilian pilot (**William Gargan**) to take the mail to Rio, but the pilot's wife (**Myrna Loy**) pleads with him not to go. Despite the dangers, the night mail is delivered on time.

The pilot despairs that his flight only meant that someone in Paris can get a postcard on Tuesday instead of Thursday, but its real value is proven when the serum is also delivered and a child is saved.

Saint Exupéry's Vol de nuit, based on real-life events in South America, had won the 1931 Prix Femina, one of the main French literary prizes (awarded by a female jury).[lxix] As a result of the prize, received widespread recognition and attention from Hollywood.

Selznick realized that Oliver H.P. Garrett's original treatment was too heavily based on "the ground" and brought in John Monk Saunders, who had worked with him on The Dawn Patrol (1930), to add more flying scenes.[lxx]

Director Clarence Brown was dissatisfied with that version, so Selznick finally called on writer Wells Root to tighten up the final draft. Brown also was interested in an accurate portrayal of aviation, as he had been a World War I pilot. Night Flight utilized both studio and location shooting with the mountainous region around Denver, Colorado, filling in for the South American Andes.[lxxi] The recently retired U.S.

Mail Douglas M-4 mail planes were featured as the Trans-Andean European Air Mail's primary aircraft.

With the success of Grand Hotel, MGM's choice of an all-star cast was intended to elevate Night Flight to epic status.[lxxii] The film's episodic style, and the various sub-plots seem to slow the pace and impede the flow. The film's action and tension are casualties of this too. After Gable's blockbuster Red Dust, this feels like a step back to a supporting role in a John Barrymore picture.

His role was really only enough to get the people in the door. He had little to do except grimly contemplate his impending demise as he is forced to ditch over water as he runs out of fuel. We see him thanks to a cockpit point of view shot. Despite the favourable reviews, however, Night Flight was considered a disappointment at the box office.[lxxiii]

Smarting from some critics' reviews of his novel, and professing that he hated the film adaptation, Saint Exupéry refused to renew his author's rights, which he had granted to MGM only for a 10-year period.[lxxiv] In 1942, Night Flight was pulled from circulation when MGM's agreement with Saint Exupéry expired.[lxxv]

The picture was finally released on DVD on June 7, 2011, over 75 years after its original release.

Dancing Lady (1933)[lxxvi]

This musical film, starring Joan Crawford and **Clark Gable**, and featuring **Franchot Tone**, (soon the next Mrs. Crawford) **Fred Astaire**, **Robert Benchley** and **the Three Stooges**. The picture was directed by **Robert Z. Leonard**, produced by John W. Considine Jr. and **David O. Selznick**, and was based on the novel of the same name by **James Warner Bellah**, published the previous year. Selznick, Louis B. Mayer's son-in-law, had been called in to augment the production department while Thalberg was on sick leave.[lxxvii] The movie had a hit song in "**Everything I Have Is Yours**", by **Burton Lane** and **Harold Adamson**.[lxxviii]

The film features the screen debut of dancer Fred Astaire, who appears as himself, as well as the first credited film appearance of **Nelson Eddy**, and an early feature film appearance of the Three Stooges – **Moe Howard**, **Curly Howard**, and **Larry Fine** – in support of the leader of their act at the time, **Ted Healy**, whose role in the films is considerably larger than theirs; the quartet is billed as "Ted Healy and His Stooges." At the other end of the comedy scale, cultured **Algonquin Round Table** humorist Robert Benchley plays a supporting role.[lxxix]

Janie Barlow (**Joan Crawford**) is a young dancer who is reduced to stripping in a burlesque show. Arrested for **indecent exposure**, she's bailed out by millionaire playboy Tod Newton (**Franchot Tone**), who was attracted to her while slumming at the theatre with his society pals. When she tries to get a part in a **Broadway musical**, Tod intercedes with director Patch Gallagher (**Clark Gable**) to get her the job: he'll put his money into the show, if Janie is given a part in the chorus. Even though he needs the money, Patch is resistant, until he sees Janie dance and realizes her talent.

When, after hard work and perseverance, Janie is elevated to the star's part – replacing Vivian Warner (**Gloria Foy**) – Tod is afraid he'll lose any chance of gaining her affection if she becomes a star, so he closes the show, and Janie, out of work, goes away with him.

Patch starts rehearsals up again using his own money, and when Janie returns and finds out that Tod has deceived her and manipulated things behind the scenes, she dumps him and joins up with her new sweetheart, Patch, to put on the show, which is a smash hit.

Dancing Lady was a box office hit upon its release and drew mostly positive reviews from critics. **Mordaunt Hall** in the **New York Times** wrote, "It is for the most part quite a lively affair.... The dancing of Fred Astaire and Miss Crawford is most graceful and charming. The photographic effects of their scenes are an impressive achievement.... Miss Crawford takes her role with no little seriousness."[lxxx]

Off the back of this success, Joan dug her heals in about a pay rise, storming off her next picture when only a few more scenes were needed. Crawford demanded an increase of $1000 a week to $4,500. If Mayer refused, she would not return to the set. Mayer agreed to $4000.[lxxxi]

That made Gable sore in more ways than one. He was on $2500 a week and Joan seemed serious about Franchot Tone and was leaving him alone.[lxxxii]

It Happened One Night (1934) Frank Capra going over the script with Colbert and Gable.

Having completed Dancing Lady with Crawford, Gable was less than impressed when they cast him in another Crawford vehicle as a gigolo. He had done enough of those parts, especially with Joan. Gable was frustrated that MGM did not have a project ready for him, probably uneasy about the prospect of being loaned out to another studio, being tied to what he viewed as a inferior project, one without his usual perks.[lxxxiii]

Gable probably had a point, it was MGM policy, especially in the 30's and 40's, to have teams of writers work on the same story ideas. That way there was never any shortage of work for their stars and each film would have the same successful elements.

This was very successful at the box-office, but hardly challenging to the actors. It was the best and worst of the studio system. The actors were churning out formula pictures with monotonous similarities. The Studio had them under contract, with most unable to choose what they would work on. Gable may have been the lion tamer at MGM, but Louis B Mayer was still the ringmaster. Always aware of the bottom line, When Columbia Pictures came to him after having trouble casting the leads for The Overland Bus (later It Happened One Night), he was happy to oblige. Gable was loaned out at $2500 a week. That gave the studio $500 profit above his contract for each week he was gone.[lxxxiv]

Gable arrived for the first day of shooting fortified against the chill of his perceived exile by a drinking binge. Interestingly, Claudette Colbert was enduring a similar punishment from Paramount. It was the director Frank Capra who brought both stars into a positive frame of mind with practical jokes and laughter, and encouraged from them a pair of award winning performances.[lxxxv]

This feat would not be equaled until One Flew Over the Cookoo's Nest (1978) and again in 1997 with As Good as it Gets, both starring Jack Nicholson.

Finally, according to Hollywood folklore, this was the film that nearly bankrupted the male underwear industry. In it Gable undresses to reveal no undershirt, the sight of the bare-chested Gable sent underwear manufacturers across the U.S. into a panic as sales figures slumped.[lxxxvi]

The popularity of this movie is based on the fact that the small town America on film liked what they saw. The initial run at the larger movie houses was okay. It wasn't until it went out to the theatres in the smaller towns that the ticket sales rocketed. It became Columbia's biggest hit to date.[lxxxvii]

Manhattan Melodrama (1934)

William Powell's stock was on the wane after years as a star at Paramount and Warner Brothers. MGM chose this crime drama to kick start his career.[lxxxviii] Gable and Loy were also added to the mix. All this combined to have it firing on all cylinders at the box-office. The whole production, headed by David O. Selznick, director Van Dyke and author Arthur Caesar found a potent mix of crime drama and fun. Also worth noting for Mickey Rooney as Blackie (Clark Gable) as a boy.[lxxxix] Powell and Loy would scale even greater heights with **The Thin Man (1934)** and it's sequels.[xc]

Men in White (1934)

In an effort to placate their star Gable was offered a serious script back at MGM, it was a character driven medical drama. For added clout Myrna Loy was at his side.[xci]
His restraint and depth in the part shows his increased range.[xcii] It proved such a success that MGM would churn out medical dramas in many guises for years to come, the most successful would be Dr. Kildare which had several film incarnations (with Lew Aryes and Lionel Barrymore), before making the move to television[xciii] (Richard Chamberlain and Raymond Massey)

Chained (1934)

The charisma and attraction of the two leads and Clarence Brown's snappy direction put the right amount of charge into this ho hum story. It paid handsome dividends at the box-office. Beneath it all, it is just a variation on the profitable Gable Crawford theme. They make it watchable just the same. The story is one we have seen before.

Diane Lovering (Crawford) and Richard Field (Otto Kruger) have been lovers for five years while Richard's wife was living overseas. When she returns and still refuses to give Richard a divorce, Diane tells him she is satisfied with their relationship as it is. But Richard insists she think it over while on a cruise to Argentina, and they can continue their relationship if she chooses if and when she returns, which she promises to do. On board the ship to Buenos Aires, she meets Mike Bradley, (Gable) who lives and has a ranch in Argentina, and they slowly fall in love. Diane returns to New York to tell Richard she fell in love, but he tells her first his wife consented to a divorce provided he will not be allowed to see his sons, and he gives her a wedding ring.

Full of guilt at his sacrifice, she marries Richard and writes Mike that she preferred the security that Richard could provide. Some time later when Mike is in New York on business, they accidentally meet. Mike senses, and she confirms, that she still loves him. They go together to confront Richard with their love, but it is not as easy as they thought it would be.[xciv]

Forsaking All Others (1934)

Forsaking All Others is a 1934 American romantic comedy-drama film directed by W.S. Van Dyke, and starring Joan Crawford, Clark Gable, and Robert Montgomery. The screenplay was written by Joseph L. Mankiewicz, which was based upon a 1933 play by Edward Barry Roberts and Frank Morgan Cavett starring Tallulah Bankhead.[xcv]

In this "comedy of errors", three friends of long standing are involved in a love triangle lasting many years. Forsaking All Others is the sixth of eight cinematic collaborations between Crawford and Gable. The plot is pretty standard fare, building on a winning formula for the two leads. Ever since Jeff Williams (**Clark Gable**) was a child, he has been in love with Mary **Clay (Joan Crawford).** Returning from Madrid, Spain, he wants to propose to her firsthand.

However, he comes to a halt, as he finds out that she is being married to Dillon 'Dill' Todd **(Robert Montgomery)** the very next day. The three had been friends since childhood, but no one besides the butler realized Jeff's feelings. So instead, he wishes all the best for the couple.

However, the next day, Dill doesn't show up to the altar, as it turns out that the night before the wedding, he **ran off** and married Connie Barnes (**Frances Drake**), a woman with whom he had had an affair in Europe some months before. Mary quickly gets out of her **wedding dress** and projects strength instead of fainting.

Although what Dill did to Mary was terrible, she still has a soft spot for him. Jeff and Mary are invited to a party at Dill and Connie's house, and the two decide to attend in order to cause some havoc and shock the newlywed couple. While the tension between Mary and Connie is palpable, Dill is shocked to see Mary. Dill and Mary share a romantic moment outside, and Connie awkwardly walks in on them. Jeff tries to smooth the situation over, but Connie remains furious.

Later, Dill calls Mary and Jeff finds out they intend to see each other. Mary knows she should not go, but the two go up to

Aunt Paula's **(Billie Burke)** country house in Phoenicia, New York. The two share a romantic day, and they profess their love for each other. Dill calls his butler to tell him to pick them up tomorrow morning, but Connie overhears and sets off for Phoenicia. Aunt Paula also realizes the two are at her house, and goes there with Jeff in order to prevent the scandal from getting worse. In fact, the night previously, Dill accidentally burned himself, and the two did not sleep together.

As Connie arrives, Jeff and Mary pretend to be a couple, but Connie does not buy it. She wants to punish Dill for his perceived unfaithfulness, while Aunt Paula wants to avoid scandal. Connie accepts a lucrative settlement and leaves for Europe, thus leaving Dill free to marry Mary. Right before the ceremony, Jeff proclaims his love for Mary and tells her that he is leaving on a boat back for the Spanish Civil War.

When the butler, Shep **(Charles Butterworth)**, tells her the cornflowers sent to her last wedding were from Jeff and not Dill, Mary realises she loves Jeff instead. She breaks off her marriage with Dill and joins Jeff on the boat—when Dill arrives at the wharf, the ship has already sailed.

This is a fast paced romantic comedy romp, today the premise may seem a little too sweet when looking at what goes up on screens today, but the energy and enthusiasm of the cast makes it fun and ever watchable. This was an undeniable hit at the box- office, with Joan Crawford leading the honourable mentions for the cast.[xcvi]

In it's day it proved very popular, reaffirming the bankability and pairing of the two stars. This film was Crawford's most financially successful film to date.[xcvii]

China Seas (1935)

1935 Saw Fox transformed and revitalised into 20th Century Fox under Darryl Zanuck. MGM netted $7.5 Million two years running and Gaumont British films successfully invaded U.S Markets with Hitchcock's 39 Steps and The Man Who Knew Too Much.[xcviii] (Eager to maintain their standing China Seas had all the star power they could muster. Plus action and romance aplenty.[xcix]

Irving Thalberg had worked on the film since 1930 when he assigned three different writers to come up with three different treatments. By 1931 Thalberg had decided on the one storyline and spent the next four years working on a script with two dozen writers, half a dozen directors and three supervisors.[c]

Here, Gable shoves off as Alan Gaskell who captains a ship bound from Hong Kong to Singapore. He's a barking sea captain with a lot on his mind. Typhoons, pirates and girls (not in that order). There's some amazing effects during the typhoon sequence, very inventive for its day and still great to watch. Mayer even tolerated that Gable risked his life by refusing a stunt double in a sequence in which he assisted numerous Chinese extras in roping in a
runaway steamroller that crashed up and down the decks of the cantilevered studio ship.[ci]

After Office Hours (1935)

This film is a newshound murder mystery enjoying a lucrative cycle of popularity at the time, which is elevated because of the leads and the amount of punch and zing cleverly injected into the dialogue by Herman Mankiewicz.[cii] That alone seems to keep this moving at a brisk pace, allowing critics and audience to happily overlook any short-comings.

The story is Hard-hitting news editor Jim Branch (Gable) falls for high-society type Sharon Norwood (Bennett) but can't get to first base as he continually makes use of her knowledge of the rich and famous to try to solve the murder of one of her socialite pals.

Call of the Wild (1935)

Jack Thornton has trouble winning enough at cards for the stake he needs to get to the Alaska gold fields. Gable was off the MGM Reservation, this time at Warner's for a frontier western based on Jack London's novel. He and Loretta Young had been on again off again relationship since the early 30's, soon after (possibly during) his affair with Joan Crawford. They rekindled their romance with this film.[ciii]

In 1935 Loretta Young also secretly gave birth to a daughter, due to her studio image and a strict morality clause in her contract, her daughter was said to be adopted.[civ] Gable had a similar clause of his own which complicated his life when he discovered he was the girl's father.

The two agreed to keep the secret and Loretta raised her as her own, frequently maintaining contact with Gable to update him on their daughter. She met her father only once, coming hurriedly home from school to find Gable and her mother chatting in the living room. Instead of going out on a date she found herself talking to Gable for hours.[cv]

Loretta went to great pains to protect both of them and their daughter from scandal, even going as far as having her ears altered when she was seven to lesson the resemblance to her father.

Though she eventually suspected it, she didn't find out for certain until after her mother's death in 2001.[cvi] In her posthumously published autobiography Loretta Young named Clark Gable as her father.

Mutiny on the Bounty (1935) AAN

This was to be a troubled production in every sense. The project was frowned upon by Louis B Mayer, as it lacked a traditional love story.

Having a Mutineer as the hero was too risky. Once more the ever-perceptive Irving Thalberg asserted himself, insisting that cruelty has always fascinated audiences. Thalberg prevailed and was vindicated by the films $4.5 Million at the Box-office. Gable made no secret about his not wanting to play Christian. His realistic style was not suited to a costume drama. His wardrobe concerns also made him question the masculinity of the character.

"The character's a pansy. And I'm not going to be seen wearing a pigtail and knickers."[cvii]

Gable made Thalberg aware of his growing concerns. He was most animated when he discovered he would have to shave his moustache in the name of realism. (It was against British Naval regulations.)[cviii] He saw his moustache as his lucky charm, something he couldn't be without in such uncharted territory.

Despite all this, in the end Gable was a professional, as well as a loyal company man. The moustache had reluctantly gone, but he would make no attempt at a British accent.[cix] With the power of Laughton's performance, that is probably wise. The lavish budget marked a significant shift after the fiscal responsibility of the Depression years. Big budget was back, so leading from the front as usual MGM made sure it was the biggest (at that time).

Much of the budget was not allocated, but came about due to a series of over runs. For starters, months of filming in the South Seas was unusable. It was underexposed. Things got further complicated when, while attempting to reshoot the footage on Catalina Island (California), a camera barge sank sending $50,000 worth of Equipment to the bottom.

This didn't help ease tensions on the set, which were far from ideal. Thalberg and the director, Frank Lloyd constantly clashed.[cx]

Gable and Laughton didn't get on, their personalities as different as their acting style. At one point Gable accused Laughton of treating him like am extra.[cxi] This says more about the different acting approaches of the two than any other obvious difference or problem between them.

Gable was less assured at this point in his career when he was challenged as an actor by other male actors. Whatever his other differences with Laughton, this was where he was most vulnerable. Likewise Laughton's uneasiness was around appearance when next to Gable.[cxii]

Gable's reactionary style was dependant on the respect of eye contact between himself and other actors in the scene.[cxiii] Laughton did not engage that way. His self-contained exploration of character added to the isolation of him. It annoyed and frustrated Gable, but it worked well for the movie and Gable rose to the challenge in his own way.

His performance stood up to Laughton, even shining alongside. Both men were nominated for awards. On a lighter note, Laughton's notoriously prickly disposition wasn't soothed by his recurrent seasickness.[cxiv]

The film succeeds today as it did when first released, winning Best Picture that year. If you like spotting famous faces in unexpected places, James Cagney pops up here in sailor garb at the start of the film. He was on suspension from Warner's because of a contract dispute and the location filming was close to his home. Frank Lloyd was an old friend and he asked for a small part in the film.[cxv]

San Francisco (1936)

This was another deliberate grand MGM undertaking. No expense spared. Both Mayer and Thalberg lavished their attention on it. Mayer was fascinated by the performance of its leading lady, Janette Macdonald, while Thalberg recognised the winning formula and mounted a production to match.[cxvi] It was a story the public liked and could easily relate to. Blackie (Gable) is a nightclub owner who finds himself re-evaluating some life choices as he falls for the good girl personified Mary Blake (Macdonald). The referee is Father Mullin (Tracy). Luckily for all concerned, everyone shines in a lavish production, along with moving singing from Macdonald. The 1906 earthquake is recreated with then groundbreaking special effects and is the final push for Blackie to turn over a new leaf when he finds Mary has survived.[cxvii] The movie and the songs were hits of the day. The film also makes the city and people of San Francisco the stars, taking on the hit song of the same name from the movie as their own.[cxviii] It was a critical and box office smash.[cxix]

The New York Times called the earthquake "a shattering spectacle" and further highlights the work of the cast as a "dramatic spectacle", touching on Tracy's turn as father Mullin as "brilliant".[cxx]

This film saw Spencer Tracy emerge as an actor of the highest caliber in his own right in the eyes of the MGM brass. The same executives noted how well Gable and Tracy worked together, using them together for a number of outings. They had a friendship built on a professional respect, that thrived on good natured competition in their scenes together, along with friendly ribbing in-between takes. For what is was worth, Gable recognized early that a picture with Tracy, meant he had to bring his A game, or Tracy would walk off with it.[cxxi]

Wife Vs Secretary (1936)

This comedy film directed and co-produced by **Clarence Brown**, again puts Harlow alongside **Clark Gable** as a successful businessman, **Jean Harlow** is his secretary, and **Myrna Loy** plays his wife, supported by **James Stewart** as the secretary's fiancé. The film was the fifth of six collaborations between Gable and Harlow and the fourth of seven between Gable and Loy.[cxxii]

The story was based on the short story of the same name by **Faith Baldwin** published in **Cosmopolitan Magazine** in May 1935.[cxxiii]

Magazine publisher Van Stanhope **(Gable)** and his wife, Linda, **(Loy)** are celebrating their third wedding anniversary. They are very much in love and Van gives Linda a diamond bracelet. However, Van's secretary, the beautiful Helen "Whitey" Wilson (**Jean Harlow**), is thought by Van's mother (**May Robson**) to be a temptation to Van.

Whitey's beau, Dave (**James Stewart**), is very uncomfortable about her relationship with Van as he calls one night while they're having dinner to ask that Whitey help him finish work at a party. Dave asks Whitey to marry him, Whitey refuses, and buries herself further in her work. Needless to say, after many misunderstandings and comical situations all ends well and Dave (James Stewart) manages to get his girl (Harlow) as well. This film would have been much harder to see the funny side of if it wasn't for the writers, director and stars who managed to spice up a pretty tired theme.[cxxiv]

The picture was the first time that Harlow and Loy worked together; they would also both appear in **Libeled Lady** later in 1936, also starring **William Powell** and **Spencer Tracy**. On Harlow during the making of Wife Vs. Secretary, Loy said, "Jean was beautiful, but far from the raucous sexpot of her films. As a matter of fact, she began to shake that image in Wife vs. Secretary.... She'd begged for a role that didn't require spouting slang and modeling lingerie. She even convinced them to darken her hair a shade, in hopes of toning down that brash image. It worked. She's really wonderful in the picture and her popularity wasn't diminished one bit. Actually we did kind of a reversal in that picture. Jean, supposedly the other woman, stayed very proper, while I had one foot in bed throughout. That's the sexiest wife I've ever played. In one scene, Clark stands outside my bedroom door and we banter, nothing more, but there's just no question about what they've done the night before. Clarence Brown, our director, made it all so subtle, yet, oh, so wonderfully suggestive. (In fact, the only vulgarity in the picture is in the breakfast scene, where I discover a diamond bracelet that Clark has hidden in the brook trout I'm about to eat. It didn't seem chic or funny to me—merely messy, typical of Hollywood's misguided notion of upper-class sophistication. I tried to get them to take it out, but they wouldn't.

Needless to say, it's the scene everyone remembers, so what do I know?). Where sex is concerned, the double entendre, the ambiguity, it seems to me, is much more effective than being too explicit. This is something the moviemakers don't seem to understand today."[cxxv]

James Stewart, meanwhile, spoke of his scene in the car with Harlow, saying, "Clarence Brown, the director, wasn't too pleased by the way I did the smooching. He made us repeat the scene about half a dozen times...I botched it up on purpose. That Jean Harlow sure was a good kisser. I realized that until then I had never been really kissed."[cxxvi]

Stewart also made mention of the film being invaluable in his education as an actor, sharing the screen with the three stars.[cxxvii] It gave him an appreciation of screen presence. Making him aware, that the projection on personality on screen was sometimes more important than being able to act.[cxxviii] Success was a combination of both.

Despite being billed sixth in the cast, Stewart enjoys the most screen time aside from the three leads, mainly romantic sequences with Harlow, including the final scene and dialogue in the movie.

Stewart made an impression in this role, where others could have easily been overwhelmed by their co-stars. He more than held his own. It wasn't lost on the critics either. The London Observer noted "Stewart acts Gable and Harlow off the screen".[cxxix] Going on to note he was clearly one to watch in the new generation coming up.[cxxx] According to MGM records the film earned $1,350,000 in the US and Canada and $717,000 elsewhere resulting in a profit of $876,000.[cxxxi]

Cain and Mabel (1936)

Cain and Mabel is a 1936 romantic comedy film designed as a vehicle for Marion Davies in which she co-stars with Clark Gable. The story had been filmed before, in 1924, by William Randolph Hearst's production company, Cosmopolitan, as a silent called The Great White Way, starring Anita Stewart and Oscar Shaw.

In this version, Robert Paige introduced the song "I'll Sing You a Thousand Love Songs", with music by Harry Warren and words by Al Dubin, who also wrote "Coney Island", "Here Comes Chiquita" and other songs.

Waitress-turned-Broadway star Mabel O'Dare (Marion Davies) and garage-mechanic-turned-prize fighter Larry Cain (Clark Gable) dislike each other intensely, but press agent Aloysius K. Reilly (Roscoe Karns) cooks up a phony romance between them for publicity. Inevitably, the two fall in love for real, and plan on getting married, with Mabel quitting show business to be a housewife and Cain quitting the fight racket to run garages in New Jersey. Naturally, their meddling friends and associated hangers on can't have that and set about sabotaging the union.

Through some twists and turns, it all ends well.

Shooting on Cain and Mabel was delayed because the part of the leading man, which eventually went to Clark Gable, had not yet been cast. Publisher William Randolph Hearst, Marion Davies' lover, convinced Warner Bros. studio head Jack L. Warner, an old friend, to get Gable from MGM as Davies' co-star.

Clark Gable had to shaved his trademark moustache for **Mutiny on the Bounty** (1935) and he went straight into this, remaining reluctantly clean shaven for this film. He had enough time to regrow his moustache for **San Francisco** (1936).[cxxxii]

Hearst wielded considerably influence on the production He spared no expense, determined Marion be showcased in a first class production. There were the elaborate musical numbers that he paid for, filmed within stage 7 (now stage 16) at Warner Brothers Studios in Burbank, California. To accommodate the enormous sets, the roof and walls of the structure were raised an additional 35 feet. The project, costing $100,000 in 1936.[cxxxiii] Despite being a financial and critical disappointment, this film's production was a great source of publicity for Warner Brothers.

The carousel used in the Coney Island sequence was built for the film at a cost of $35,000. Marion Davies kept it for her Santa Monica home after filming wrapped.[cxxxiv]

Sheilah Graham, a syndicated entertainment columnist, reported that raising the stage 35 feet in height took four weeks (with 200) workers, and cost $300,000.[cxxxv] Graham also reported the set of the climactic "Thousand Love Songs" number was lit by 600 arc lights, bringing temperatures to 110 degrees inside the stage. Marion Davies had over one hundred pounds of ice trucked in throughout the filming of the number in order to make filming easier for the dancers. The chorus sat on it. A total of 225 dancers were used for the "Thousand Love Songs" musical number.[cxxxvi] The film awed enough in this area to receive an Academy Award Nomination for Best Dance Direction for Bobby Connolly.[cxxxvii]

That was the only sparkle on a horrendously overblown production, it did little to halt Marion's career slide. That said, by all accounts she was well liked by all who worked with her and had a gift for light comedy that is best enjoyed in her earlier films. Here, try as she might, she was ill at ease and a little the worse for wear. Hearst knew Marion was drinking more now, despite his best efforts, he was unable to curtail her consumption on this film.[cxxxviii]

The film was a box-office office flop to say the least. Warner's would have pulled the pin on it and their relatively new contract to distribute Cosmopolitan's (Marion Davies) films, had it not been for the fact that Hearst personally covered some 3 million dollars of the film's elaborate overruns. The New York Times called it a "colossus of incongruity."[cxxxix]

Hearst himself was beginning to feel the pinch by 1937, so the last vehicle for Miss Davies Ever Since Eve (1937) was a much more modestly produced affair. It hardly mattered, audiences chose to remember her earlier work. Ever Since Eve left much more quietly than its predecessor, bringing down the curtain on the career of Marion Davies and Cosmopolitan Pictures, much to the relief of her friends and admirers at Warner Brothers.[cxl]

Love On the Run (1936)

Everyone was back on familiar ground here. **Joan Crawford**, **Franchot Tone**, and **Clark Gable** in a story about rival newspaper **correspondents** assigned to cover the marriage of a **socialite** (Crawford). In the sure hands of **W. S. Van Dyke** and produced by **Joseph L. Mankiewicz**. Love on the Run keeps the pace of the action, laughs and dialogue brisk for all concerned. In this, the seventh of eight cinematic collaborations between Crawford and Gable, all sorts of silliness takes place as two rival reporters chase the story and the same girl. The fans were happy to see Gable and Crawford up to their old tricks and it proved a popular hit.[cxli] The critics noticed the premise wearing a little thin. The production was good enough to cover up any potential holes. Howard Barnes of the **New York Herald Tribune** wrote, "A lot of gay nonsense has been strung together ... a fantastic and insubstantial narrative, with the result that it is almost continuously amusing and frequently hilarious ... Miss Crawford, of the big eyes and flowing hair, turns in a surprisingly volatile and amusing performance as the heiress." John T. McManus in his review for **The New York Times**, said it was "A slightly daffy cinematic item of absolutely no importance." **Variety** wrote that among other things it had several vapid moments."

According to MGM records Love on the Run earned $1,141,000 in the United States and Canada and $721,000 elsewhere resulting in a profit of $677,000.

Saratoga (1937)

Saratoga is a 1937 American **romantic comedy film** written by **Anita Loos** and directed by **Jack Conway**. **Clark Gable** and **Jean Harlow** team up in their sixth and final film collaboration, also featuring **Lionel Barrymore, Frank Morgan, Walter Pidgeon, Hattie McDaniel,** and **Margaret Hamilton**.[cxlii] Harlow and Gable had proven their onscreen chemistry in a string of movies, including Red Dust (1932), China Seas (1935) and, Wife vs. Secretary (1936).

In the film, Harlow plays Carol Clayton, the daughter of an incorrigible gambler, who loses his fortune (a lucrative horse farm), to his good friend and bookmaker, Duke Bradley (Clark Gable). At the time of the transaction, Frank Clayton (Jonathan Hale), vows that he will never allow his daughter to become involved in the seedy side of the track. Soon after, Hale dies and Carol sets about regaining her birthright. The complications follow as Carol is Attracted to Duke, while being with a nice respectable fellow. (Pidgeon)

Jean Harlow died before filming was finished, and it was completed using stand-ins. Saratoga was **MGM**'s biggest money maker of 1937.

Screenwriter Robert Hopkins originally intended the script to be a vehicle for Harlow, but the studio at first attempted to borrow **Carole Lombard** from **Paramount Pictures** to star with real life love interest Gable.[cxliii] After this, it was reported that **Joan Crawford** would play Harlow's role, but by 1937, Harlow was reported as the star. Walter Pidgeon was borrowed from **Universal** for the film.

At the time of filming, Harlow was recovering from oral surgery to remove impacted wisdom teeth. **Paul Bern**, her second husband had committed suicide and she had just divorced director **Harold Rosson**, her third, after just one year of marriage. Harlow was now with **William Powell**, and wanted to marry him. When filming of Saratoga was 90% completed, Harlow collapsed on the set during a scene with Walter Pidgeon and died about a week later, of **kidney failure**.[cxliv]

MGM wanted to reshoot the movie with **Virginia Bruce** or **Jean Arthur**, but Harlow's fans complained, so the remaining scenes were filmed with **Mary Dees**, shot from behind or with costumes that obscured her face, playing Harlow's part for the camera, and **Paula Winslowe** supplying Harlow's voice.[cxlv]

The film was released on July 23, 1937, not quite seven weeks after Harlow's death, and the crowds of her fans that turned out to see the film, turning it into one MGM's big hits for 1937.[cxlvi]

Parnell (1937)

Irving Thalberg had died, after a period of mourning the studio returned to production. Two high quality vehicles got the full MGM treatment. The first **Captains Courageous** for Spencer Tracy from Rudyard Kipling's story, the second a lavish period political drama following Ireland's struggle for self rule led by Charles Stewart Parnell.[cxlvii] Myrna Loy would provide the romance of the piece, as his mistress.

Clark Gable would headline the production as Parnell. Mayer took a great deal of personal interest in the production from beginning to end. His eye for quality shows in the end product, but no amount of dedicated dazzle could distract from Gable's performance.[cxlviii] It wasn't that bad, it was awful. Despite best efforts the film comes off as too wordy and dull.[cxlix] The quest for realism even saw Randolph Churchill (Winston's Father) used as a member of Parliament. When asked about the filming experience he noted he made more money as an MGM member of Parliament than he did as a real one.[cl]

As filming began, Gable felt very uneasy with his role, either unable or unwilling to portray the sensitive nature required to capture the character. Loy later recalled, "I learned about another side of him at that time. He was a man who loved poetry and fine literature, read it, and knew it. He would read poetry to me sometimes during breaks, but he didn't want anyone to know it."[cli]

One of the many concerns that Gable had about this production, added to literally everything about it, was the acting that would be required of him to play out a believable death scene. During the filming of the death scene, Stahl put on mood music to help the actors get into character. Gable loathed the music and complained to Carole Lombard. Lombard was never one to miss an opportunity for a laugh. The next day, when Stahl called for the music to be turned on, a jazzy version of "I'll Be Glad When You're Dead, You Rascal You", went floating throughout the studio.[clii]

Gable may have viewed it as a personal setback in his quest to better himself as an actor, but with his usual good humour seemed to simply move on to the next project.

The fans barely noticed either, but rumour has it that Spencer Tracy never missed a chance to playfully needle his colleague. It was one of the few flops of both Gable's and Loy's careers.

The King   1938

The Industry was facing another slump, profits were again down across the board, but MGM was still on top with 10 million dollars.[cliii] Gable too seemed to go from strength to strength.

This was the year Ed Sullivan, through his national newspaper column, had him crowned the 'King' of Hollywood.[cliv] Some 20 million readers were surveyed and also asked to name a Queen, Myrna Loy.

Personally, Gable was in an emotional quandary similar to 1931. By 1938 He had renewed his acquaintance with Carole Lombard, moving in with her while still married to Ria.[clv] Into this mix came an offer to Clark Gable of Rhett Butler and Vice a Versa.

Test Pilot (1938)

Gable was on a roll. To capitalise on his pairing with Myrna Loy as King and Queen of Hollywood, MGM produced a series of high quality scripts with top-notch productions to back them up. This was the first. It would become one of the biggest hits in MGM history.[clvi]

The combination of action, drama, romance and excellent special effects proved to be almost too much excitement for some reviewers, as they happily kissed the ground after enduring such a high flying thriller.

Newsweek commented that under Fleming's direction the performances are the real thing and just the prescription the ailing box-office needs.[clvii] *Time* called the flying shots of the movie "among the best ever staged in cinema"[clviii]

Too Hot to Handle (1938)

Is about a **newsreel** reporter, the woman he is attracted to, and his fierce competitor, played by **Clark Gable**, **Myrna Loy**, and **Walter Pidgeon** respectively. Many of the comedy gags and faked newsreel stories were devised by an uncredited **Buster Keaton**.[clix]

Myrna Loy enjoyed her fourth on-screen pairing with Clark Gable in Too Hot to Handle (1938); the previous three were Manhattan Melodrama in 1934, the disastrous biopic Parnell in 1937 and Test Pilot earlier in 1938. This time out Walter Pidgeon took Spencer Tracy's role as the other contender for Loy's affections. Gable and Pidgeon play rival newsreel cameramen who bury their differences to help aviatrix Loy find her brother, lost in the Amazon jungle, only to ignite a new competition over her.[clx]

Too Hot to Handle was very much a typical studio product for its era. Although the adventure covered action in China and Brazil, the crew never left the back lot. The film movies at such a break neck pace, you don't have time to take in any inaccuracies. Jack Conway is at the helm here, a specialist in action and comedy who had previously put Loy through her paces in the hit comedy Libeled Lady (1936).[clxi]

For history buffs, the films take on the frantic life of newsreel photographers, often manufacturing events with which to sell their work has a nice authenticity to it, thanks to two people on the film previously working as newsreel men themselves. Len Hammond, who wrote the film's original story, and Laurence Stallings, who co-wrote the screenplay, had worked for Fox Movietone news, happy to call on their own experience to flesh the story out.[clxii]

Too Hot to Handle would be the final teaming for Gable and Loy. During World War II, she would take an extended leave from MGM and the movies to do her part for the war effort. Loy discovered later that during the scene in which Gable pulls her out of a burning crashed plane, special effects technicians lost control of the fire, but Gable went ahead with the scene, pulling her to safety as scripted.

Loy only found out when the story was in newspapers around the country, never entirely sure whether she was in danger or the story was manufactured to sell the picture.[clxiii]

This brisk film had it all, action, Romance, Humour and Gable with Myrna Loy. It would prove to be a potent combination at the Box office as well.[clxiv]

Idiot's Delight (1938)

The last item on 1938's production schedule was noted for containing Gable's only musical number, he obviously enjoys his only dance number ever put to film. The story was part play, part Hollywood, with the bits in-between tailored to showcase Shearer and Gable, also by the playwright (Robert E. Sherwood).[clxv]

It has a new beginning to flesh out the love story, with the middle section straight from the play, plus the obligatory revamped Hollywood happy ending.[clxvi] He plays a hoofer stuck in a Continental hotel as World War 2 begins. He encounters a striking European entertainer who underneath it all could be an entertainer he fell for years earlier. The meaty and complex role here is Shearer's. Although she seems to be channeling Garbo in some scenes, mostly is up to the task.

The production is flashy and finishes the production year of with a bang under Clarence Brown's able direction.

Gable Rules

Gone With The Wind, a book Gable hadn't even read. The part was uncertain territory for him, so he turned it down. Soon public opinion would over take him, eliminating all other contenders.[clxvii]

But he didn't think he was suited to the part. As with Mutiny on the Bounty, he was not sure he could pull it off.

"It wasn't I didn't appreciate the compliment the public was paying me. It was simply that Rhett was too big an order. I didn't want any part of him..."[clxviii]

Rhett Butler was another complex challenging character. When he finally read the book Gable was no closer to finding an affinity with his character. As well as his own doubts about his ability, the production itself was a mammoth undertaking. There was so much press coverage.

Personal and financial pressures were mounting. Clark Gable was now openly living with Carole Lombard while still married to Ria, the producers and the studio were justifiably concerned about any negative press this would create. They had too much riding on this. Gable still wouldn't budge.

"There's going to be six million eyes on me, all daring me to fail." [clxix]

There were family politics of another kind at work here too. Selznick was Mayer's son in law, but keeping it in the family was not reason enough to loan Gable out to a project he was so hostile to.[clxx] Gable was banking on Mayer putting too higher price on his head for the loan out. There always had to be a good deal in it for Metro. The fact Mayer was not keen to loan out his star just added another layer of negotiation to the whole project.

In truth, David was not immediately enamored with it. Civil War movies as a genre had been a dog at the box office until now.[clxxi] Gone With The Wind would soon become the relatively new studios eighth production.[clxxii]

Selznick would finally be swayed by a combination of persistent forces that included the head of his New York story office, Kay Brown who peppered and pummeled her boss with memos and telegrams in the hope of wearing him down. Keen to succeed in her offensive, she opened on another front. A copy of the book was sent to one of Selznick's key financial backers at the young studio.[clxxiii]

Four weeks after the book was published in June 1936, to immediately fervent sales, David O Selznick bought the film rights for $ 50,000.[clxxiv] It was quite an achievement for a first time author. Book sales would pass 1 million copies in six months.[clxxv] Later Selznick felt compelled to give the author another $50,000 which he felt was more in keeping with its popularity.[clxxvi]

He had hoped to go it alone with his dream project, but casting was a major hurdle. First, a poll put Clark Gable at 98% preferred actor for the role of Rhett, and Gable was tightly held by Metro and his father in law, Louis B Mayer.[clxxvii]

Negotiations would be hard. He also didn't have a leading lady that could really be Scarlett. Even after the immensely popular find Scarlett campaign, there was no easy solution. He was trying to avoid his father in law by securing a distribution deal with Warner's, but that didn't solve his Gable problem. He would have to speak to MGM. This gifted Mr. Mayer one of his biggest business deals, plus it put Gable firmly on the hook too.

First Mayer used the situation to his best advantage while appealing to Gable's marital survival instinct, via his bank balance. He suggested the studio would happily pay Ria an ample settlement rumoured to be $286,000 so Clark and Carole could marry.[clxxviii] Of course there was a sizeable string attached, it would tie him down as Rhett Butler.[clxxix] Clark Gable and Carol Lombard married in San Diego o March 29th 1939.[clxxx] Gable signed the contract in August 1938.[clxxxi]

For Gable's work on the production and an investment of $1,250,000 (less than a third of the film's total cost) Mayer secured distribution rights and 50% of the profits.[clxxxii]

Once the December premiere was over, the recently married happy couple would settle in to routine of work, friends and one another that was far removed from both their burgeoning careers.

It was to be at once a hectic, happy and idyllic time. But ominously across the other side of the world storm clouds were brewing. The clouds brought with them a tragedy too close to home. But whatever happens, for now and forever Gone With The Wind has a life of its own.

Gone With the Wind (1939) AAN

Gable was not the only one who felt trapped by GWTW. Leslie Howard was railroaded by the pressure of audience expectation, plus lack of work.[clxxxiii] Like Gable, he saw the endorsement of all and sundry as reason to avoid it at all costs.

"I am suspicious that fifty million Americans can't be right!"
[clxxxiv]

Frugal optimism fuelled his procrastination in accepting. Ashley Wilkes held out a lucrative purse, while Leslie Howard hoped for any other more challenging offer. Finally, overcome by his bank balance and boredom, (plus the promise of producing *Intermezzo* [clxxxv]) he relented.[clxxxvi]
Throughout, Leslie never read the book and often wished he didn't have to read the script. He managed to keep a straight face as he took his money and ran.

For those who still don't know anything about the movie or the book, I'll try and keep it brief. Gone with the Wind was adapted from **Margaret Mitchell**'s **Pulitzer**-winning **1936 novel**. It was produced by **David O. Selznick** of **Selznick International Pictures** and directed by **Victor Fleming**.

Set in the 19th-century American South, it is the story of **Scarlett O'Hara**, the strong-willed daughter of a Georgia plantation owner, from her romantic pursuit of **Ashley Wilkes**, who is married to his cousin, **Melanie Hamilton**, to her marriage to **Rhett Butler**.

Against the backdrop of the **American Civil War** and **Reconstruction era**, the story is told from the perspective of rich white Southerners. The leading roles are **Vivien Leigh** (Scarlett), **Clark Gable** (Rhett), **Leslie Howard** (Ashley), and **Olivia de Havilland** (Melanie).

The production of the film was a mammoth undertaking from the start.

Filming was delayed for two years due to Selznick's determination to secure Gable for the role of Rhett Butler, and the "search for Scarlett" led to 1,400 women being interviewed for the part.[clxxxvii] Selznick's maniacal obsession with each detail of production kicked in early.

The original screenplay was written by **Sidney Howard,** but underwent many revisions by several writers in an attempt to get it down to a suitable length. It started out at 5 and a half hours screen time and ran 400 pages.[clxxxviii] A change was needed. Selznick wanted Howard to remain on the set to make revisions but Howard refused to leave New England, so revisions were handled by a host of local writers.

Selznick dismissed director George Cukor three weeks into filming and sought out Victor Fleming (The Wizard of Oz). Fleming was unhappy with the script, so Selznick brought in famed writer **Ben Hecht** to rewrite the entire screenplay within seven days. Hecht was in the middle of working on the film **At the Circus** for the **Marx Brothers**. When he was awakened by a frantic Selznick and Fleming and told he had to start the Gone with the Wind rewrite. Selznick was already five weeks in to shooting.

Selznick was losing $50,000 each day the film was on hold waiting for a rewrite.[clxxxix]

Hecht Recalled the episode in a letter to screenwriter friend **Gene Fowler**, Selznick and director Fleming could not wait for him to read the novel. To save time and meet the ludicrous 7 day deadline. They would act out scenes based on Sidney Howard's original script.

Hecht wrote, "After each scene had been performed and discussed, I sat down at the typewriter and wrote it out. Selznick and Fleming, eager to continue with their acting, kept hurrying me. We worked in this fashion for seven days, putting in eighteen to twenty hours a day. Selznick refused to let us eat lunch, arguing that food would slow us up. He provided bananas and salted peanuts ... thus on the seventh day I had completed, unscathed, the first nine reels of the Civil War epic."[cxc]

Hecht returned to Howard's original draft and by the end of the week had succeeded in revising the entire first half of the script. Selznick undertook rewriting the second half himself but fell behind schedule, so Howard returned to work on the script for one week, reworking several key scenes in part two.

Despite the number of writers and changes, the final script was remarkably close to Howard's version. The fact that Howard's name alone appears on the credits may have been as much a gesture to his memory as to his writing, for in 1939 Sidney Howard died at age 48 in a farm-tractor accident, and before the movie's premiere.[cxci]

The casting of the two lead roles became a complex, two-year undertaking. For the role of Rhett Butler, Selznick wanted **Clark Gable** from the start, but Gable was under contract to MGM, who rarely loaned him to other studios. **Gary Cooper** was considered, along with Ronald Coleman.[cxcii] Warner's offered a package of their stars in exchange for distribution, so that was too rich for Selznick, who wanted to maintain control.

Selznick was more determined to get Gable than ever and eventually struck a deal with MGM. Selznick's father-in-law, MGM chief Louis B. Mayer, offered in August 1938 to provide Gable and $1,250,000 for half of the film's budget but for a high price: Selznick would have to pay Gable's weekly salary, and half the profits would go to MGM while **Loew's, Inc**—MGM's parent company—would release the film.[cxciii]

The arrangement to release through MGM meant delaying the start of production until the end of 1938, when Selznick's distribution deal with **United Artists** concluded. Selznick used the delay to continue to revise the script and, more importantly, build publicity for the film by **searching for the role of Scarlett**. Selznick began a nationwide **casting call** that interviewed 1,400 unknowns.[cxciv] The effort cost $100,000 and was useless for the film, but created invaluable publicity.

Early frontrunners included **Miriam Hopkins** and **Tallulah Bankhead**, who were regarded as possibilities by Selznick prior to the purchase of the film rights; **Joan Crawford**, who was signed to MGM, was also considered as a potential pairing with Gable. Actresses, including Jean Arthur and Paulette Goddard remained under consideration by December 1938; however, only two finalists, Paulette Goddard and Vivien Leigh, were tested.

Selznick had been aware of Vivien Leigh, a young English actress who was still little known in America, for the role of Scarlett since February 1938 when Selznick saw her in **A Yank at Oxford**. For Leigh's part, she had set her mind on winning the role and with the help of her husband Laurence Olivier, they quickly laid the ground work. She was quick to sign with an appropriately connected American agency in London. The **Myron Selznick** talent agency (headed by David Selznick's brother, one of the owners of Selznick International), and she had requested that her name be submitted for consideration as Scarlett.[cxcv] By the summer of 1938 the Selznick's were negotiating with **Alexander Korda**, to whom Leigh was under contract, for her services later that year.[cxcvi] Selznick's brother arranged for them to meet for the first time on the night of December 10, 1938, when the burning of Atlanta was filmed.[cxcvii]

In a letter to his wife two days later, Selznick admitted that Leigh was "the Scarlett dark horse", and after a series of screen tests, her casting was announced on January 16, 1939.[cxcviii]

George Cukor was selected to direct, but his previously good working relationship with Selznick did not stop him from being fired shortly after filming had begun, despite having spent almost two years in pre-production on Gone with the Wind.

He was replaced by Victor Fleming, who in turn was briefly replaced by **Sam Wood** while Fleming took some time off due to exhaustion.

It has been suggested Cukor was replaced to please Gable. He was an old friend, so he was pleased, but his departure probably owes more to Selznick disagreeing with the vision Cukor had in mind. That and it was David's show.[cxcix] Besides, Gable had worked successfully with Cukor in Manhattan Melodrama (1934). When filming for Gone With The Wind started Gable had little filming responsibilities in the first few weeks of production. It was split into two parts that also roughly reflected the division of directing duties.

Most of the filming was done on "**the back forty**" of Selznick International with all the location scenes being photographed in California, in **Los Angeles County** or **Ventura County**. Tara, existed only as a plywood and papier-mâché facade built on the California studio lot.[cc] For the burning of Atlanta, other false facades were built in front of the "back forty's" many abandoned sets, with Selznick himself at the controls for the explosives that burned them down.[cci]

It was during this sequence that a bit of movie folklore was neatly staged by clever conspirators, providing a spontaneous chance meeting between Selznick and Vivien Leigh, to secure her the role she so desperately wanted.[ccii]

Myron, Selznick's brother and head of the agent representing Vivien Leigh in America, knew his brother well enough to know of his fondness of fateful encounters. Together all involved played this one well.[cciii]

Others were not as fortunate. Gable was tied to tidy up his personal life and was almost over whelmed by expectations. Leslie Howard thought the whole prospect preposterous but needed the money.[cciv] Olivia De Havilland had to make her case with Warner Brothers boss Jack Warner, so she could be released to do an audition for the part of Melanie for Selznick. Initially he refused, Olivia smartly taking her case to Mrs. Warner. Olivia was permitted to do the film.[ccv]

Principal photography began January 26, 1939, and ended on July 1, with post-production work continuing until November 11, 1939. Cukor continued privately to coach Leigh and De Havilland.[ccvi]

Gable's experience on the film started inauspiciously. He was kept waiting for an hour and a half as he waited to meet Vivien Leigh for the first time at a photo shoot at the grand staircase.

"I'll walk off this picture if she's going to behave like that." He fumed. Unseen, she had over heard. She came out and walking up to him and said "I quite agree Mr. Gable, if I were a man I'd tell Vivien Leigh to go straight back to England and fuck herself." Gable's anger immediately left him, he was disarmed and charmed and relaxed immediately.[ccvii]

Vivien's unexpectedly colourful and candid vocabulary was often deployed in her frustrations as she continued to work on the picture. Once Cukor was removed she would frequently clash with both Selznick and new director Fleming over bringing Scarlett to life on film as in the book.

Gable remained wary of her, they came from very different beginnings as actors, but while Gable was the well-established star, her theatre grounding gave her a confidence in attacking and assuming the difficult and challenging parts of her role that Gable did not possess. He continued to struggle with living up to his character's heroic image.[ccviii]

Gable remained above it all until the now famous scene where he was required to cry on camera. Always conscious of his hard won image, as well as the misfire of the costume drama Parnell, he was not about to compromise it with unmanly tears. Carole Lombard pointed out he had always known it was in the script. In the end it was his friendship with Fleming that the director was able to use to break the impasse. He could film two versions, one with tears and one without. Gable would have final say. Seeing the results, Gable relented and wept on film.[ccix]

Gable only noticeably felt the strain on one other occasion, as Vivien Leigh recalled. It was the scene where Rhett carries a kicking and screaming Scarlett up the big staircase to the bedroom.

Fleming started filming it late in the afternoon and the scene had to be repeated over and over. Finally Fleming called for one more take and a nearly spent Gable picked her up and trod up the stairs again. Fleming thanked Clark before adding "I really didn't need that shot. I just had a little bet on you couldn't make it."[ccx]

It was a long and involved shoot, but with Scarlett in the majority of scenes, the difference in workload was telling. Vivien Leigh had worked 125 days, Gable 71, Olivia 59 and Leslie 32.[ccxi]

Selznick's relentless pace combined with a maniacal obsession with detail made the filming arduous for all, especially when combined with so many other strong personalities. The film received positive reviews upon its release in December 1939, with some noting it seemed dramatically lacking and bloated.[ccxii] The casting was praised, many reviewers found Vivien Leigh especially suited to her role as Scarlett.[ccxiii]

At the 12th Academy Awards, it received ten Awards (eight competitive, two honorary) from thirteen nominations, including wins for Best Picture, Best Director (Victor Fleming), Best Adapted Screenplay (posthumously awarded to Sidney Howard), Best Actress (Vivien Leigh) and Best Supporting Actress (**Hattie McDaniel**, becoming the first African-American to win an Academy Award)[ccxiv]. It set records for the total number of wins and nominations at the time.

Sources at the time put the estimated production costs at $3.85 million, making it the second most expensive film made up to that point. Ben Hur (1925) cost more.[ccxv]

Test Screening and Premiere

On September 9, 1939, Selznick, his wife, **Irene**, investor **John "Jock" Whitney** and film editor Hal Kern drove out to **Riverside, California** to preview it at the **Fox Theatre**. The film was still a **rough cut** at this stage, It ran for four hours and twenty-five minutes, but would later be cut down to under four hours for its proper release.

A double bill of **Hawaiian Nights** and **Beau Geste** was playing, and after the first feature it was announced that the theater would be screening a preview; the audience were informed they could leave but would not be readmitted once the film had begun, nor would phone calls be allowed once the theater had been sealed. When the title appeared on the screen the audience cheered, and after it had finished it received a standing ovation.[ccxvi]

Gable and Lombard at the premiere,

December 1st 1939

About 300,000 people came out in Atlanta for the film's premiere at the **Loew's Grand Theatre** on December 15, 1939. It was the climax of three days of festivities hosted by Mayor **William B. Hartsfield**, which included a parade of limousines featuring stars from the film, receptions, thousands of Confederate flags and a costume ball.[ccxvii]

Eurith D. Rivers, the governor of Georgia, declared December 15 a state holiday. An estimated three hundred thousand residents and visitors to Atlanta lined the streets for up to seven miles to watch a procession of limousines bring the stars from the airport. Premieres in New York and Los Angeles followed, the latter attended by some of the actresses that had been considered for the part of Scarlett, among them Paulette Goddard, Norma Shearer and Joan Crawford.

Leigh would go on to win in the Best Actress category for her performance at the **1939 New York Film Critics Circle Awards**. Of Clark Gable's performance as Rhett Butler, critics wrote the characterization was "as close to Miss Mitchell's conception—and the audience's—as might be imagined".[ccxviii]

Of the other principal cast members, Leslie Howard was said to be "convincing" as the weak-willed Ashley, with Olivia de Havilland a "standout" as Melanie.[ccxix] Hattie McDaniel's performance as Mammy was also singled out by many critics. Hattie McDaniel became the first African-American to win an Academy Award—beating out her co-star Olivia de Havilland who was also nominated in the same category.[ccxx]

Its record of eight competitive wins stood until **Gigi** (1958) won nine, and its overall record of ten was broken by **Ben Hur** (1959) which won eleven.

The running time for Gone with the Wind is just under 221 minutes, however, including the **overture**, **intermission**, **entr'acte**, and exit music, Gone with the Wind lasts for 234 minutes (although some sources put its full length at 238 minutes).ccxxi

Sidney Howard became the first **posthumous** Oscar winner (Screenplay) and Selznick personally received the **Irving G. Thalberg Memorial Award** for his career achievements.

Crowd Pleaser

Gone with the Wind broke attendance records everywhere. At the **Capitol Theatre** in New York alone, it was averaging eleven thousand admissions per day in late December, and within four years of its release had sold an estimated sixty million tickets across the United States—sales equivalent to just under **half the population at the time**.

It repeated its success overseas, and was a sensational hit during **the Blitz** in London, opening in April 1940 and playing for four years. By the time MGM withdrew it from circulation at the end of 1943 its worldwide distribution had returned a **gross rental** (the studio's share of the box office gross) of $32 million, making it the **most profitable film ever made up to that point**.

The bulk of the earnings from Gone with the Wind came from its road show and first-run engagements, which represented 70 percent and 50 percent of the box-office gross respectively, before entering general release (which at the time typically saw the distributor's share set at 30–35 percent of the gross).

Gable was well aware of the films impact on his career, commenting that the films re-releases were the main reason for his enduring success as a movie star.[ccxxii]

From December 1939 to July 1940, the film played only advance-ticket **road show** engagements at a limited number of theaters at prices upwards of $1—more than double the price of a regular first-run feature—with MGM collecting an unprecedented 70 percent of the box office receipts (as opposed to the typical 30–35 percent of the period).

After reaching saturation as a roadshow, MGM revised its terms to a 50 percent cut and halved the prices, before it finally entered general release in 1941 at "popular" prices.

Along with its distribution and advertising costs, total expenditure on the film was as high as $7 million.[ccxxiii]

Later releases

In 1942, Selznick liquidated his company for tax reasons, and sold his share in Gone with the Wind to his business partner,

John Whitney, for $500,000. In turn, Whitney sold it on to MGM for $2.8 million, so that the studio more or less owned the film outright.

MGM immediately re-released the film in spring 1942, and again in 1947 and 1954. The 1954 reissue was the first time the film was shown in **widescreen**, compromising the original **Academy ratio** and cropping the top and bottom to an aspect ratio of 1.75:1. In doing so, a number of shots were optically re-framed and cut into the three-strip camera negatives, forever altering five shots in the film.

A 1961 release commemorated the **centennial** anniversary of the start of the Civil War, and included a gala "premiere" at the Loew's Grand Theater. It was attended by Selznick and many other stars of the film, including Vivien Leigh and Olivia de Havilland; Clark Gable had died the previous year.

For its 1967 re-release, it was blown up to **70mm**, and issued with updated poster artwork. There were further re-releases in 1971, 1974 and 1989. For the fiftieth anniversary reissue in 1989, it was given a complete audio and video restoration. It was released theatrically one more time in the United States, in 1998.

In 2013, a **4K digital restoration** was released in the United Kingdom to coincide with Vivien Leigh's centenary.

In 2014, special screenings were scheduled over a two-day period at theaters across the United States to coincide with the film's 75th anniversary.

The film received its world television premiere on the **HBO** cable network on June 11, 1976, and played on the channel for a total of fourteen times throughout the rest of the month. It made its **network television** debut in November later that year: **NBC** paid $5 million for a one-off airing, and it was broadcast in two parts on successive evenings. It became at that time the **highest-rated television program** ever presented on a single network, watched by 47.5 percent of the households sampled in America, and 65 percent of television viewers, still the record for the highest rated film to ever air on television.

In 1978, **CBS** signed a deal worth $35 million to broadcast the film twenty times over as many years.[ccxxiv] **Turner Entertainment** acquired the MGM film library in 1986, but the deal did not include the television rights to Gone with the Wind, which were still held by CBS. A deal was struck in which the rights were returned to Turner Entertainment and CBS's broadcast rights to The Wizard of Oz were extended.[ccxxv] It was used to launch two cable channels owned by Turner Broadcasting :**Turner Network Television** (1988) and **Turner Classic Movies** (1994).[ccxxvi]

It debuted on **videocassette** in March 1985, where it placed second in the sales charts, and has since been released on **DVD** and **Blu-ray Disc** formats.

The bottom line

The re-release in 1947 earned an impressive $5 million rental in the United States and Canada, and was one of the top ten releases of the year. Successful re-releases in 1954 and 1961 enabled it to retain its position as the industry's top earner, it was finally overtaken by **The Sound of Music** in 1966.

The 1967 reissue was unusual in that MGM opted to road show it, a decision that turned it into the most successful re-release in the history of the industry. It generated a box-office gross of $68 million, making it MGM's most lucrative picture after **Doctor Zhivago** from the latter half of the decade.

MGM earned a rental of $41 million from the release, with the U.S. and Canadian share amounting to over $30 million, placing it second only to **The Graduate** for that year. Including its $6.7 million rental from the 1961 reissue, it was the fourth highest-earner of the decade in the North American market, with only The Sound of Music, The Graduate and Doctor Zhivago making more for their distributors.

A further re-release in 1971 allowed it to briefly recapture the record from The Sound of Music, bringing its total worldwide gross rental to about $116 million by the end of 1971—more than trebling its earnings from its initial release—before losing the record again the following year to **The Godfather**.[ccxxvii] By 1974, its estimated rentals were over $150 Million.[ccxxviii]

Across all releases, it is estimated that Gone with the Wind has sold over **200 million tickets in the United States and Canada**, and 35 million tickets in the United Kingdom, generating more theater admissions in those territories than any other film. It remains, with inflation adjustments, the most successful film in history.[ccxxix]

In total, Gone with the Wind has grossed over $390 million globally at the box office; in 2007 Turner Entertainment estimated the gross to be equivalent to approximately $3.3 billion when adjusted for inflation to current prices, while Guinness World Records arrived at a figure of $3.44 billion in 2014.[ccxxx]

The film remains immensely popular with audiences into the 21st century, having been voted the most popular film in two nationwide polls of Americans undertaken by Harris Interactive in 2008, and again in 2014.[ccxxxi]

Gone With The Wind is widely regarded as the peak of epic golden years of Hollywood movie making. One of the greatest of all time it has placed in the top ten of the **American Film Institute**'s list of **top 100 American films** since the list's **inception in 1998**, and in 1989, the United States **Library of Congress** selected it for preservation in their **National Film Registry**.ccxxxii

It became the highest-earning film made up to that point, and remains one of the most successful films in box-office history.

At time of writing, just two surviving credited cast members remain from the film: Centenarian Olivia de Havilland, who played Melanie Wilkes and Mickey Kuhn, who played her son Beau Wilkes.ccxxxiii

---

Intermission

Select Bibliography

Anderson, J. *History of Movie Comedy.* Deans International Publishing. London. 1985.

Bellamy, Ralph. *When the smoke hit the fan.* Double Day & Co. New York. 1979

Bergan, R, Fuller, G, Malcolm, D. *Academy Award Winners 1927 to the Present.* Prion. London. 1994.

Bridges, H. & Boodman, T.C. *Gone With The Wind. The definitive illustrated history of the Book, The Movie, and The Ledgend.* Simon & Schuster 1989.

Callow, S. *Charles Laughton. A Difficult Actor.* Methuen London Ltd. 1987 (1988 Edition)

Carey,G. Doug & Mary. A *Biography of Douglas Fairbanks and Mary Pickford.* E.P. Dutton New York. 1977.

Cohen, Daniel & Susan. *500 Great Films* 1987 Exeter Books. Bison Book Group.

Deschner, D. *The films of Spencer Tracy.* The Citadel Press, Secaucus, New Jersey. 1968 (Second Paperbound Printing 1973)

Douglas Eames, J & Bergman, R. The MGM Story. Hamlyn, London 1993 Edition.

Finler, J.W. The Hollywood Story. Octopus Books. London 1988.

Fairbanks Jnr, D. *Salad Days An Autobiography.* Fontana/Collins 1988 (1989 Edition)

Fox-Sheinwood, P. Gone but not Forgotten. Bell Publishing Co. New York. 1981

Fox-Sheinwood, P. Too Young to Die. Treasure Press. Ottenheimer Publishers. USA 1991 Edition.

Grant, N. Clark Gable In his own words. Hamlyn Publications 1992 Edition.

Gwinn, A. (editor) Entertainment Weekly The 100 Greatest Stars of all time. Time Inc. Home Entertainment. 1997 (1999 Edition)

Harris, Warren G. Clark Gable, A Biography. London: Aurum Press, 2002

Higham, C. Merchant of Dreams. Louis B. Mayer. MGM and the secret of Hollywood. Sidgwick & Jackson. London 1993.

Hirschhorn, J. Rating the Movie Stars for Home Video, T.V, Cable Publications International Limited Illinois. 1983.

Howard, L. R. A Quite Remarkable Father. Longmans Green and Co. Ltd, London. 1959 (1960 Ed. Second Impression).

Hutchinson, Ivan. Ivan Hutchinson's Movies on TV and Video. The Five Mile Press, Balwyn Victoria (Aust). 1992

Karney, R. & Finler, J.W. (Editors) Cinema Year by Year 1894-2001. A Dorling Kindersley Book. London 2001.

Lloyd, A & Robinson,D. Movies of the Silent Years. Orbis, London 1984 (1985 Edition)

Medved, Harry & Michael. The Hollywood Hall of Shame. The most expensive flops in movie history. Angus & Robertson Publishers (Australia) 1984.

Norman, B. The Hollywood Greats Arrow Books Limited London. 1979 (1988 Edition)

Scherman, D. E. (Editor) Life Goes To The Movies. Time-Life Books New York. 1975

Schneider, Steven Jay. (General Editor) 1001 Movies You Must See Before You Die. A Quintet Book. Published by ABC books for The Australian Broadcasting Corporation, GPO Box 9994 Sydney NSW 2001. Quintet Publishing 2003. (2004 Edition.)

Shipman, D. The Great Movie Stars: The Golden Years. Hamlyn London. 1970. (1979 Edition)

Spada, J. Grace. The Secret Lives of a Princess. Sidgwick & Jackson London 1987 (Second Edition)

Walker, Alexander. VIVIEN. The Life of Vivien Leigh. Grove Weidenfeld, New York, New York. 1991 Edition.

Walker, J. (Editor) Halliwell's filmgoer's companion 10th Ed. Harper Collins Publisher's 1993.

Glimpse of Gable
Filmography

Prelude
(As extra or Bit Part)
1. White Man 1924
2. Forbidden Paradise 1924
3. The Social Exile 1925
4. The Merry Widow 1925
5. The Plastic Age 1925
6. North Star 1925
7. The Pacemakers 1925
8. The Johnstown Flood 1926

1930-31
9. The Painted Desert 1931 *

10. The Easiest Way 1931
11. Dance fools dance 1931
12. The Finger points 1931
13. The Secret 6 1931
14. Laughing sinners 1931
15. A free soul 1931
16. Sporting blood 1931
17. Night Nurse 1931
18. Susan Lennox, her fall and rise 1931
19. Possessed 1931
20. Hell Divers 1931

Clark Gable, Movie Star

21. Polly of the Circus 1932
22. Red Dust
23. No Man Of Her Own
24. Strange interlude
25. The White Sister 1933
26. Hold Your Man
27. Night Flight
28. Dancing Lady
29. It Happened One Night (1934) AA Peter Warne
30. Men in White
31. Manhattan Melodrama
32. Chained
33. Forsaking All Others
34. After Office Hours (1935)
35. China Seas
36. Call of the Wild
37. Mutiny on the Bounty AAN Fletcher Christian
38. Wife vs Secretary (1936)
39. San Francisco
40. Cain and Mabel
41. Love on the Run
42. Parnell (1937)
43. Saratoga

The King

44. Test Pilot (1938)

45. Too Hot to Handle
46. Idiot's Delight
47. Gone With the Wind (1939) AAN Rhett Butler (1939)

About the Author: Lhmoviebuff@yahoo.com.au

Lachlan has a passion for the movies that began at the age of 4. At 13 Mum gave him an old Royal portable typewriter and writing about anything and everything began. He has reviewed Movies on radio, in print and online since 1996. Now working freelance, He divides his time between family and writing.

Lachlan published his first book on the film teaming of Jack Lemmon & Walter Matthau: **Team Work** in 2001.

Endnotes and Image credits

Overview

[i] Grant, N. Clark Gable In his own words. Hamlyn Publications 1992 Edition.

[ii] Hatari 1962 http://www.imdb.com/title/tt0056059/trivia (accessed 16.02.16)

[iii] http://www.imdb.com/title/tt0056059/trivia?ref_=tt_trv_trv (accessed 16.12.15)

[iv] loc. cit.

[v] loc.cit.

[vi] loc.cit.

[vii] http://www.encyclopedia.com/topic/Clark_Gable.aspx (accessed 16.02.16)

[viii] loc.cit.

[ix] loc.cit.

[x] loc.cit.

Prologue 1901-1930

[x] Grant, N. Clark Gable In his own words. Hamlyn Publications 1992 Edition.

[xi] loc cit.

[xii] Douglas Eames, J & Bergman, R. The MGM Story. Hamlyn, London 1993 Edition. p66

[xiii] Grant, N. Clark Gable In his own words. Hamlyn Publications 1992 Edition. loc.cit.

[xiv] loc.cit.

[xv] loc.cit.

[xvi] Finler, Joel W. The Hollywood Story. Octopus Books, London. 1988 p21

[xvii] Finler, ibid., p20.

[xviii] Walker, J. (Editor) Halliwell's filmgoer's companion 10th Ed. Harper Collins Publisher's 1993 p 305

The Painted Desert

[xix] Shipman, David. The Great Movie Stars. The Golden Years. Angus & Robertson Publishers 1979 p222.

[xx] Grant, N. Clark Gable In his own words. Hamlyn Publications 1992 Edition.

[xxi] Bellamy, R. When the Smoke Hits the Fan. Double Day and Co. 1979 pp 111-112

[xxii] Douglas Eames, J & Bergman, R. The MGM Story. Hamlyn, London 1993 Edition. p7

[xxiii] loc.cit.

[xxiv] https://en.wikipedia.org/wiki/The_Easiest_Way (accessed 19.02.16)

Dance Fools, Dance

[xxv] Higham, C. Merchant of Dreams. Sidgwick & Jackson, London. 1993 p165

[xxvi] loc.cit. p 169

[xxvii] https://en.wikipedia.org/wiki/The_Finger_Points (accessed 20.02.16)

[xxviii] https://en.wikipedia.org/wiki/Wallace_Beery (accessed 19.02.16)

[xxix] loc.cit.

[xxx] loc.cit.

[xxxi] Fairbanks, D. Jnr. Salad Days

[xxxii] Grant, N. Clark Gable In his own words. Hamlyn Publications 1992 p8

A Free Soul

[xxxiii] https://en.wikipedia.org/wiki/A_Free_Soul (accessed 23.02.16)

[xxxiv] Howard,L.R. A Quite Remarkable Father. Longman's 1960 Ed. p 172

[xxxv] ibid., p157-58

[xxxvi] https://en.wikipedia.org/wiki/Sporting_Blood (accessed 23.02.16)

Susan Lenox (Her fall and Rise)

[xxxvii] Higham, C. Merchant of Dreams. Sidgwick & Jackson. London. 1993. P 170

[xxxviii] https://en.wikipedia.org/wiki/Susan_Lenox_(Her_Fall_and_Rise) (accessed 23.02.16)

[xxxix] https://en.wikipedia.org/wiki/Greta_Garbo#cite_note-166 (accessed 23.02.16)

[xl] Higham, C. Merchant of Dreams. Sidgwick & Jackson. London 1993. Pp 169-70

[xli] Douglas Eames, J & Bergman, R. The MGM Story. Hamlyn, London 1993 Edition. p74

[xlii] Higham, C. Merchant of Dreams. Sidgwick & Jackson. London 1993. P170

[xliii] Grant, N. Clark Gable In his own words. Hamlyn Publications 1992. p 23

[xliv] ibid., p11

Possessed

[xlv] https://en.wikipedia.org/wiki/Possessed_(1931_film) (accessed 23.02.16)

[xlvi] Fairbanks, D. Jnr. Salad Days

Hell Divers

[xlvii] https://en.wikipedia.org/wiki/Hell_Divers#Production (accessed 23.02.16)

Polly of the Circus

[xlviii] Grant, N. Clark Gable In his own words. Hamlyn Publications 1992. p 21

[xlix] loc.cit.

[l] Higham, C. Merchant of Dreams. Sidgwick & Jackson. London 1993. p173

[li] loc.cit.

[lii] ibid., p 72

[liii] http://www.nytimes.com/movie/review?res=9D01E2D91F3FE633A2575AC1A9659C946394D6CF (accessed 29.02.16)

[liv] Higham, C. Merchant of Dreams. Sidgwick & Jackson. London 1993. p174

[lv] https://en.wikipedia.org/wiki/Red_Dust (accessed 23.02.16)

No Man of Her Own

[lvi] https://en.wikipedia.org/wiki/No_Man_of_Her_Own_(1932_film) (accessed 26.02.16)

[lvii] loc.cit.

[lviii] loc.cit.

[lix] Douglas Eames, J & Bergman, R. The MGM Story. Hamlyn, London 1993 Edition. p82

Strange Interlude

[lx] Ibid., p 85

[lxi] loc.cit.

The White Sister

[lxii] https://en.wikipedia.org/wiki/The_White_Sister_(1933_film) (accessed 29.02.16)

[lxiii] Ibid., p90

[lxiv] ibid., p 91

Night Flight

[lxv] https://en.wikipedia.org/wiki/Night_Flight_(1933_film)) accessed 26.02.16

[lxvi] Douglas Eames, J & Bergman, R. The MGM Story. Hamlyn, London 1993 Edition. p82

[lxvii] http://www.warnerbros.com/studio/news/locked-vault-more-75-years-lost-mgm-classic-%E2%80%9Cnight-flight%E2%80%9D-arrives-dvd-first-time-june-7 (accessed 26.02.16)

[lxviii] loc.cit.

[lxix] loc.cit.

[lxx] https://en.wikipedia.org/wiki/Night_Flight_(1933_film)) accessed 26.02.16

[lxxi] loc.cit.

[lxxii] Ibid., p 98

[lxxiii] loc.cit.

[lxxiv] http://pre-code.com/night-flight-1933-review-john-barrymore-clark-gable/ (accessed 26.02.16)

[lxxv] loc.cit.

Dancing Lady

[lxxvi] https://en.wikipedia.org/wiki/Dancing_Lady (accessed 01.04.16)

[lxxvii] Douglas Eames, J & Bergman, R. The MGM Story. Hamlyn, London 1993 Edition. p 97.

[lxxviii] Loc.cit.

[lxxix] Loc.cit.

[lxxx] Hall, Mordaunt. "Joan Crawford, Clark Gable and Franchot Tone in the Capitol's New Pictorial Offering" New York Times (December 1, 1933)

[lxxxi] Higham, C. Merchant of Dreams. Sidgwick & Jackson. London 1993. P 211

[lxxxii] loc.cit.

It Happened One Night

[lxxxiii] Harris 2002 pp 112-114.

[lxxxiv] loc.cit.

[lxxxv] loc.cit.

[lxxxvi] Higham, C. ibid., p 220

[lxxxvii] https://en.wikipedia.org/wiki/It_Happened_One_Night#cite_note-29 (accessed 01.03.16)

Manhattan Melodrama

[lxxxviii] Douglas Eames, J & Bergman, R. The MGM Story. Hamlyn, London 1993 Edition. p 103.

Men In White

[lxxxix] loc.cit

[xc] Douglas Eames, J & Bergman, R. ibid., p 104.

[xci] loc.cit.

[xcii] loc.cit.

[xciii] loc.cit

Chained

[xciv] https://en.wikipedia.org/wiki/Chained_(1934_film) (accessed 01.03.16)

Forsaking All Others (1934)

[xcv] https://en.wikipedia.org/wiki/Forsaking_All_Others (accessed 01.03.16)

[xcvi] https://en.wikipedia.org/wiki/Forsaking_All_Others retrieved 15. 12.15

[xcvii] loc.cit.

China Seas

[xcviii] Douglas Eames, J & Bergman, R. The MGM Story. Hamlyn, London 1993 Edition. p 109

[xcix] ibid., p 114

98 Scott Eyman, Lion of Hollywood: The Life and Legend of Louis B. Mayer, Robson, 2005 p 155-156

[ci] Higham, C. Merchant of Dreams. Sidgwick & Jackson. London 1993. p 265

After Office Hours

[cii] Douglas Eames, J & Bergman, R. The MGM Story. Hamlyn, London 1993 Edition. p 116

Call of the Wild

[ciii] https://en.wikipedia.org/wiki/The_Call_of_the_Wild_(1935_film) (accessed 02.03.16)

[civ] http://www.imdb.com/title/tt0026164/trivia?ref_=tt_trv_trv (accessed 02.03.16)

[cv] http://www.imdb.com/name/nm0507395/bio?ref_=nm_ov_bio_sm (accessed 02.03.16)

[cvi] loc.cit.

Mutiny on the Bounty

[cvii] Grant, N. Clark Gable In his own words. Hamlyn Publications 1992 Edition. p28

[cviii] Higham, C. Merchant of Dreams. Ibid., p 233

[cix] Douglas Eames, J & Bergman, R. The MGM Story. Hamlyn, London 1993 Edition. p 119.

[cx] Higham, C. Merchant of Dreams. Sidgwick & Jackson. London 1993. P 237

[cxi] loc.cit.

[cxii] Callow, S. Charles Laughton. A Difficult Actor. Methuen London Ltd. 1987 (1988 Edition) pp 98-99

[cxiii] loc.cit.

[cxiv] Higham, C. Merchant of Dreams ibid., 237

[cxv] https://en.wikipedia.org/wiki/Mutiny_on_the_Bounty_(1935_film) (accessed 02.03.16)

San Francisco

[cxvi] Higham, C. Merchant of Dreams. Ibid., p 244

[cxvii] Douglas Eames, J & Bergman, R. The MGM Story. ibid., p 125

[cxviii] loc.cit.

[cxix] loc.cit.

[cxx] Deschner, D. The films of Spencer Tracy. The Citadel Press, Secaucus, New Jersey. 1968 (Second Paperbound Printing 1973) pp 130-131

[cxxi] Grant, N. Clark Gable In his own words. ibid., p26

Wife Versus Secretary

[cxxii] https://en.wikipedia.org/wiki/Wife_vs._Secretary (accessed 07.03.16)

[cxxiii] loc.cit.

[cxxiv] Douglas Eames, J & Bergman, R. The MGM Story. ibid., p 126

[cxxv] https://en.wikipedia.org/wiki/Wife_vs._Secretary (accessed 07.03.16)

[cxxvi] loc.cit.

[cxxvii] Thomas, Terry. A Wonderful Life. The Films and Career of James Stewart. Citadel 1990 Ed. pp 34-35.

[cxxviii] loc.cit.

[cxxix] loc.cit.

[cxxx] loc.cit.

[cxxxi] https://en.wikipedia.org/wiki/Wife_vs._Secretary (accessed 07.03.16)

Cain and Mabel

[cxxxii] http://www.imdb.com/title/tt0027413/trivia?ref_=tt_trv_trv (accessed 08.03.16)

[cxxxiii] loc.cit.

[cxxxiv] Medved, Harry & Michael. The Hollywood Hall of Shame. The most expensive flops in movie history. Angus & Robertson Publishers (Australia) 1984. p 41

[cxxxv] http://www.imdb.com/title/tt0027413/trivia?ref_=tt_trv_trv (accessed 08.03.16)

[cxxxvi] loc.cit.

[cxxxvii] http://www.imdb.com/title/tt0027413/awards?ref_=tt_awd (accessed 08.03.16)

[cxxxviii] Medved, Harry & Michael. ibid., p38

[cxxxix] http://www.nytimes.com/movie/review?res=9B0CE3DB163EEE3BBC4152DFB667838D629EDE (accessed 08.03.16)

[cxl] Medved, Harry & Michael. ibid., p38

Love on the Run

[cxli] Douglas Eames, J & Bergman, R. The MGM Story. ibid., p 127

Saratoga

[cxlii] Douglas Eames, J & Bergman, R. The MGM Story. ibid., p 131

[cxliii] http://www.tcm.com/tcmdb/title/531/Saratoga/articles.html (accessed 20.03.16)

[cxliv] loc.cit.

[cxlv] http://www.jeanharlow.com/about/biography.html (accessed 20.03.16)

[cxlvi] Which Cinema Films Have Earned the Most Money Since 1947?". The Argus (Melbourne, Vic. : 1848 - 1956) (Melbourne, Vic.: National Library of Australia). 4 March 1944. p. 3 Supplement: The Argus Weekend magazine. (accessed 20.03.16)

Parnell

[cxlvii] Higham, C. Merchant of Dreams. Ibid., pp 256-57

[cxlviii] loc.cit.

[cxlix] Douglas Eames, J & Bergman, R. The MGM Story. ibid., p 133

[cl] loc.cit.

[cli] http://www.tcm.com/tcmdb/title/2488/Parnell/articles.html (accessed 15.03.16)

[clii] http://www.tcm.com/tcmdb/title/2488/Parnell/trivia.html (accessed 15.03.16)

The King

[cliii] Douglas Eames, J & Bergman, R. The MGM Story. ibid., p 138

[cliv] Grant, N. Clark Gable In his own words. ibid., p26

[clv] Grant, N. Clark Gable In his own words. ibid., p20

Test Pilot

[clvi] Douglas Eames, J & Bergman, R. The MGM Story. ibid., p 145

[clvii] Deschner, D. The films of Spencer Tracy ibid., p 146

[clviii] loc.cit.

Too Hot to Handle

[clix] https://en.wikipedia.org/wiki/Too_Hot_to_Handle_(1938_film) (accessed 08.03.16)

[clx] http://www.tcm.com/tcmdb/title/1620/Too-Hot-to-Handle/articles.html (accessed 17.03.16)

[clxi] Deschner, D. The films of Spencer Tracy ibid., pp 132-3

clxii http://www.tcm.com/tcmdb/title/1620/Too-Hot-to-Handle/articles.html (accessed 17.03.16)

clxiii loc.cit.

clxiv Douglas Eames, J & Bergman, R. The MGM Story. ibid., p 145

Idiot's Delight

clxv Douglas Eames, J & Bergman, R. The MGM Story. ibid., p 145

clxvi loc.cit.

Gable Rules

clxvii Douglas Eames, J & Bergman, R. The MGM Story. ibid., p 152

clxviii Bridges, H & Boodman, Terryl, C. Gone with the Wind. The definitive illustrated history of the book, the movie, and the legend. Simon & Schuster. Great Britain. 1989. P16

clxix Grant, N. Clark Gable In his own words. ibid., p 32

clxx Bridges, H. & Boodman, T.C. ibid., p16

clxxi Bridges, H & Boodman, Terryl, C. Gone with the Wind. ibid., p9

clxxii loc.cit.

clxxiii loc.cit.

clxxiv Douglas Eames, J & Bergman, R. The MGM Story. ibid., p 152

clxxv loc.cit.

clxxvi loc.cit.

clxxvii Bridges, H. & Boodman, T.C. ibid., p16

clxxviii Bridges, H. & Boodman, T.C. ibid., p25

clxxix http://www.destinationhollywood.com/movies/gonewiththewind/feature_didyouknow.shtml (accessed February 12, 2016)

clxxx Higham, C. Merchant of Dreams. Ibid., p 291

clxxxi Bridges, H. & Boodman, T.C. ibid., p 25.

clxxxii Douglas Eames, J & Bergman, R. The MGM Story. ibid., p 152

Gone With The Wind

clxxxiii Howard, L.R. A Quite Remarkable Father. ibid., p 234

clxxxiv loc.cit.

clxxxv Howard,L.R. A Quite Remarkable Father. Ibid., p 241

clxxxvi Bridges, H. & Boodman, T.C. ibid., p 40

clxxxvii Bridges, H. & Boodman, T.C. ibid., p 17

clxxxviii Bridges, H. & Boodman, T.C. ibid., pp 24-25

clxxxix Bridges, H. & Boodman, T.C. ibid., p 57

[cxc] MacAdams, William. Ben Hecht. New York: Barricade Books (1990) pp. 199–201.
[cxci] Douglas Eames, J & Bergman, R. The MGM Story. ibid., p 152
[cxcii] Bridges, H. & Boodman, T.C. ibid., p 16.
[cxciii] Higham, C. Merchant of Dreams. Ibid., pp 283-284.
[cxciv] Bridges, H. & Boodman, T.C. ibid., p 17
[cxcv] Walker, Alexander. VIVIEN. The Life of Vivien Leigh. Grove Weidenfeld, New York, New York. 1991 Edition. p. 110
[cxcvi] Walker, Alexander. VIVIEN. The Life of Vivien Leigh. Ibid., pp. 117-118
[cxcvii] Walker, Alexander. VIVIEN. The Life of Vivien Leigh. Ibid., pp. 112-113
[cxcviii] Walker, Alexander. VIVIEN. The Life of Vivien Leigh. Ibid., p. 119
[cxcix] Walker, Alexander. VIVIEN. The Life of Vivien Leigh. Ibid., p. 122
[cc] Molt, Cynthia Marylee (1990). Gone with the Wind on Film: A Complete Reference. Jefferson, NC: McFarland & Company. 1990 pp. 272–281.
[cci] Molt, Cynthia Marylee (1990). Gone with the Wind on Film: A Complete Reference. Jefferson, NC: McFarland & Company. pp. 272–281.
[ccii] Bridges, H. & Boodman, T.C. ibid., p 26
[cciii] Walker, Alexander. VIVIEN. The Life of Vivien Leigh. Ibid., p. 112-113.
[cciv] Howard, L.R. A Quite Remarkable Father. ibid., p 234
[ccv] Bridges, H. & Boodman, T.C. ibid., p 40
[ccvi] Walker, Alexander. VIVIEN. ibid., p. 124
[ccvii] Walker, Alexander ibid., pp. 122-3
[ccviii] loc.cit.
[ccix] Bridges, H. & Boodman, T.C. ibid., pp 187-188
[ccx] loc.cit.
[ccxi] Bridges, H. & Boodman, T.C. ibid., p 204
[ccxii] Flinn, John C., Sr. (December 20, 1939). "Gone With the Wind". Variety. Archived from the original on February 24, 2013. Retrieved March 26 2016.
[ccxiii] Nugent, Frank S. (December 20, 1939). "The Screen in Review; David Selznick's 'Gone With the Wind' Has Its Long-Awaited Premiere at Astor and Capitol, Recalling Civil War and Plantation Days of South--Seen as Treating Book With Great Fidelity". The New York Times. Retrieved March 26 2016.
[ccxiv] Cohen, Daniel & Susan. 500 Great Films 1987 Exeter Books. Bison Book Group p88
[ccxv] Cinema: G With the W". Time. December 25, 1939. pp. 1–2 & 7. Retrieved March 26 2016.
[ccxvi] "Gone with the Wind (1939) – Notes". TCM database. Turner Classic Movies. Retrieved January 16, 2013.
[ccxvii] Bridges, H. & Boodman, T.C. ibid., pp213-225

ccxviii Flinn, John C., Sr. (December 20, 1939). "Gone With the Wind". Variety. Archived from the original on February 24, 2013. Retrieved March 24 2016).

ccxix loc.cit.

ccxx Haskell, Molly (2010). Frankly, My Dear: Gone With the Wind Revisited. Icons of America. Yale University Press. pp. 213–214.

ccxxi Kim, Wook (February 22, 2013). "17 Unusual Oscar Records – Longest Film (Running Time) to Win an Award: 431 Minutes". Time. Retrieved March 24, 2016.

ccxxii Grant, Neil, ibid., p32

ccxxiii Shearer, Lloyd (October 26, 1947). "GWTW: Supercolossal Saga of an Epic". The New York Times. Retrieved March 24 2016)

ccxxiv Bartel, Pauline (1989). The Complete Gone with the Wind Trivia Book: The Movie and More. Taylor Trade Publishing. pp. 64–69, 127 & 161–172

ccxxv loc.cit

ccxxvi Clark, Kenneth R. (September 29, 1988). "Tnt Rides In On 'Gone With Wind'". Chicago Tribune. Retrieved January 29, 2013.

ccxxvii Kramer, Peter (2005). The New Hollywood: From Bonnie And Clyde To Star Wars. Short Cuts 30. Wallflower Press. p. 46

ccxxviii Douglas Eames, J & Bergman, R. The MGM Story. ibid., p 152

ccxxix Highest box office film gross – inflation adjusted". Guinness World Records. 2014. Retrieved February 9, 2015.

ccxxx loc.cit.

ccxxxi Shannon-Missal, Larry (December 17, 2014). "Gone but Not Forgotten: Gone with the Wind is Still America's Favorite Movie" (Press release).Harris Interactive. Archived from the original on December 28, 2014. Retrieved February 13, 2015.

ccxxxii Miller, Frank; Stafford, Jeff. "Gone with the Wind (1939) – Articles". TCM database. Turner Classic Movies. Archived from the original on September 26, 2013.

ccxxxiii Noland, Claire (April 8, 2014). "Mary Anderson dies at 96; actress had role in 'Gone With the Wind'". Los Angeles Times. Retrieved April 8,2014.

Image Credits

istock photos (Front Cover)

Red Dust (Corbis)
It Happened One Night (Corbis)
Mutiny on the Bounty   (Corbis)
Gone With The Wind   (Corbis)
Gone With The Wind premiere (Corbis)
istock photos (Back Cover)